RAYS *of the*
SAME LIGHT

RAYS *of the* SAME LIGHT

PARALLEL PASSAGES, WITH COMMENTARY,
FROM THE BIBLE AND THE BHAGAVAD GITA

——— Volume Three ———

J. Donald Walters

Crystal Clarity, Publishers
14618 Tyler Foote Road
Nevada City, CA 95959

Cover design by Bella Potapovskaya
Cover photo by J. Donald Walters

This work is lovingly dedicated
to my great spiritual teacher,
Paramhansa Yogananda

Other books by the same author:

Crises In Modern Thought
The Reappearance of Christ
Rays of the Same Light, Volume II
Cities of Light
Intentional Communities
The Artist as a Channel
The Art of Supportive Leadership
Education for Life
The Search

Contents

Introduction
to Volume Three

This work presents a few of the essential truths that unite two of the great Scriptures of the world: the Bible and the Bhagavad Gita.

The Bible, of course, needs no introduction to Western readers. Westerners may be helped, however, by a few introductory words about the Bhagavad Gita.

This beautiful poem is unquestionably the best-known Scripture in India. It contains the essence of the teachings of the ancient *Vedas* and *Upanishads*, and is the most complete exposition of the Hindu religion to be found in any single volume.

Christian missionaries in India were struck from their first introduction to this noble work by its many similarities to the teachings of Jesus Christ — so much so that some of them decided its teachings must have been borrowed from the New Testament. The truth is, the Bhagavad Gita was already widely known in India centuries before Christ.

This precedence in time, however, in no way

signifies that Jesus, instead, was indebted to that Indian scripture for his teachings. The very thesis of the present work is that truth is one. Those great souls who have taught from the realization of truth have not needed the Scriptures to instruct them in it. God Himself has been their Teacher.

Similarities between the great Scriptures of the world are, therefore, inevitable. One would hardly expect God to contradict Himself! It is mankind, rather, who sets one religion against another, and creates division where only unity and harmony were intended.

Where, indeed, is the great master — the Jesus Christ, the Krishna, the Buddha — who ever denounced another master? The only people they ever reprimanded were those who clung stubbornly to materialism — never, certainly, those who earnestly sought, and still less those who taught from, divine insight.

The teachings of the masters are universal. Their unvarying goal has been to lead people out of the narrow prison of selfhood into the eternal freedom of Spirit.

In the present work, I have tried to show that this eternal message touches human life on every level, even the most mundane. In keeping with the practical wisdom of those great masters, I have tried to bring their teachings to a level of understanding to which modern man can relate.

Preface
to Volume Three

As I stated in the introduction to Volume One of this work, these commentaries are based on the teachings of the great master Paramhansa Yogananda, whose direct disciple I have the great good fortune to be. It is important that the reader know the genesis of the commentaries, and the authority on which they are based.

For none but a great master has the spiritual right to express himself on the deeper aspects of Scripture. No one, in other words, has the divine authority to speak or write beyond his own inner experience of Truth.

This work is not a simple report of Yogananda's Scripture commentaries. Indeed, I have made it a point, in the writing of it, to refer to his commentaries only lightly. It would have been pointless to duplicate them.

Forty years of discipleship have, however, brought me a certain attunement with the core of his teachings. It is from that central understanding that these commentaries have been written.

Basic to the mission of Paramhansa Yogananda in the West, and indeed to the life work of the great masters by whom he was sent here, was to show the underlying similarity between the Holy Bible, particularly the teachings of Jesus, and the teachings of Krishna in the Bhagavad Gita. This being his major work on earth, it is the duty of his disciples to further that work.

A central truth can be expressed and applied in countless ways, each of them relevant to the needs of different people. The function of the disciple is not merely to quote his teacher verbatim, but to apply the teacher's writings creatively, from his own inner attunement and experience, with a view to demonstrating ever more broadly their relevance to human needs.

What I have sought to do in the present work is bring the deep, intuitive insights of Paramhansa Yogananda to a level of common experience. What I have contributed to the Master's mission, also, is to pair specific Bible and Gita passages, in order the more clearly to highlight their similarities.

The first volume of this work was given another name: *The Reappearance of Christ.* This reference to Christ, however, proved too esoteric for most readers. By *Christ* I did not mean Jesus, but the eternal Christ Consciousness, which has reappeared repeatedly on earth — through Jesus, through Krishna, and through many other great masters, including, in our times, Paramhansa Yogananda.

These Scriptural selections were designed for reading and study in sets of two, one pair at a time, each week of the year. The period covered in this final volume corresponds roughly to the months of September through December.

Part VI

The Importance of Right Attitude

Secrets of
Self-Transformation

Bible

Blessed Are the Inwardly Free

This passage is from the gospel of St. Matthew, Chapter 5, Verses 1-3:

"And seeing the multitudes, he went up into a mountain: and when he was set, his disciples came unto him:

"And he opened his mouth, and taught them, saying,

"Blessed are the poor in spirit: for theirs is the kingdom of heaven."

Commentary

Thus begins Jesus' "Sermon on the Mount," the first ten verses of which are separately known as the Beatitudes.

Jesus was speaking here to his close disciples, not

to the masses. "Seeing the multitudes," we read, "he went up into a mountain: and when he was set, his disciples came unto him." What he taught that day went far beyond simple moral preachment. He was addressing devotees whose deep desire was not to live a God-*fearing* life on earth, merely, but a God-*loving* one: those who wanted to dwell constantly in the consciousness of God.

Religious people generally feel that they have "fought the good fight" if they can manage to "be good, do good, and stay out of mischief." A sermon satisfies them if it exhorts them to be truthful and fair in their dealings with others, and to "do unto others as they would be done by." Jesus, out of very compassion, rarely challenged such basically good people to aspire to heights for which they were not yet prepared. When alluding publicly to higher truths, he usually spoke, as the Bible tells us, in parables.

That he also recognized higher levels of truth, however, is obvious. Hence his frequently voiced hint, "He that hath ears to hear, let him hear."

The Beatitudes were addressed to those who sought deeper teaching on the soul's relationship with God. His teaching here is uncompromising in its summons to spiritual perfection.

The key to understanding the Beatitudes lies in that simple word from which their name is derived: "blessed."

"Blessed are the poor in spirit." How easy it is for critics to interpret the words, "poor in spirit," negatively! In modern speech, indeed, "to show poor spirit" means to be a poor loser. Want of spirit suggests, besides, lack of courage or will power. Even when this Beatitude is taken in a positive sense, as of course it was intended, to the modern ear it seems lacking in force. Was Jesus referring merely to an absence of vainglory? If so, the virtue he praised is essentially passive, and not greatly inspiring.

Yet Jesus said that the poor in spirit are "blessed." Blessedness implies a state of exaltation. Surely, this word cannot in any way be associated with passivity. Obviously, Jesus meant these words in another sense altogether.

There is a second key to understanding the Beatitudes. It lies in the specific blessing promised with each of them.

In the first Beatitude, the blessing promised was the kingdom of heaven. Heaven, as Jesus normally used the word, referred to the highest goal of spiritual striving: union with God. Such a state of perfection has been attained by a few great saints, but certainly not by the great majority of Christians. It is much more exalted than the heaven to which most people aspire — a place of sensory beauty and happiness after death.

Jesus was speaking clearly, for example, of union with God in his famous parable of the mustard seed. "The kingdom of heaven," he said, "is like to a grain of mustard seed." (Matthew 13:31) The seed grows to become a mighty tree, "so that the birds of the air come and lodge in the branches thereof." As an allegory for the state to which good people go after death, this comparison is bewildering. As an allegory, however, of the soul's expansion in the Spirit, it is beautiful, clear, and straightforward.

Most people think of heaven as an idealized version of this world. They imagine it as a place of verdant meadows, sunny vales, peaceful streams — a place where, tradition says, "cool breezes blow evermore."

Is this belief a merely wishful fantasy? The Scriptures of many religions state that such a place actually exists. Numerous saints, besides, have beheld this heaven in their visions. A few of them claim even to have entered it during states of ecstasy. This sensorily pleasing heaven, however, is not the goal of those who deeply long for union with God.

An Indian saint once reprimanded a wealthy philanthropist for directing all his energies toward the performance of outward charities. "To be sure," he assured the man, "your good works will earn you a place in heaven. But is that really all you want? Infinitely greater are the blessings that await you in God. Compared to His bliss, happiness in heaven is like contenting oneself with a mere nibble of sweetness, out of a vast field of sugar cane!

"If you truly want to please God," continued the saint, "purify yourself of ego-attachments. Meditate daily. Offer yourself up to Him in deep, silent inner communion. Discover yourself inwardly as an expression of His infinite light."

God wants nothing less from us, His children, than our complete and unconditional love. Jesus, in the Sermon on the Mount, was addressing his disciples, who deeply accepted this truth. "Surrender yourselves," he urged them, "on the altar of God's love!"

On other occasions he referred also to the astral heaven (as it is also known). He described it as tradition does: a place of reward for the virtuous. He referred also to hell, a place where evil deeds must be expiated.

The Indian Scriptures have a word for this operation of divine justice: *Karma*, they call it. According to karmic law, they insist, every action — mental as well as physical — attracts to itself automatic (because self-completing) consequences. St. Paul referred to this law when he wrote to the Galatians, "Be not deceived; God is not mocked: for whatsoever a man soweth, that shall he also reap." (Galatians 6:7)

The highest heaven, however, to which Jesus referred more frequently, lies beyond ego-motivated action. Soul-union with God is not attainable by good deeds, merely — except to the extent that good deeds help one to develop perfect love.

St. Paul expressed this thought also when he wrote that man is saved not by works, but by faith. (Ephesians 2:8,9) Faith comes as a result of perfect openness to God.

"Blessed are the poor in spirit: for theirs is the kingdom of heaven." Jesus was urging his disciples to accept the thought of man's *nothingness* before God, and of God's "everythingness." Poverty of spirit, to him, meant a glorious lack, not a passive one. To be "poor in spirit" means to be completely without ego, and without selfish desires, but utterly receptive to God's will.

St. John of the Cross expressed the same thought in one of his mystical poems:

"In order to arrive at being everything,
    Desire to be nothing.
In order to arrive at the knowledge of everything,
    Desire to know nothing."

In each of the Beatitudes, Jesus offered not merely moral, but the highest spiritual, teaching. Underlying them all was his undeviating message: God wants from us our unconditional love. This truth, to which Jesus' entire life bore testimony, is the highest, and indeed the only true, goal in life.

Thus, through the Holy Bible, God has spoken to mankind.

Bhagavad Gita

Blessed Are the Free in Spirit

This passage is from the third Chapter, the 27th
and 28th Stanzas, in the poetic translation of Sir
Edwin Arnold:

"All things are everywhere by Nature
wrought
In interaction of the qualities.
The fool, cheated by self, thinks, 'This I did'
And 'That I wrought'; but — ah, thou strong-
armed prince! —
A better-lessoned mind, knowing the play
Of visible things within the world of sense,
And how the qualities must qualify,
Standeth aloof even from his acts."

Commentary

Krishna describes Arjuna as "strong-armed." Dispassion, in other words, is not a passive quality. It demands the greatest mental vigor, iron determination, and perfect clarity as to one's soul-priorities.

A certain disciple of Paramhansa Yogananda's used to relate the story of his first meeting the Master. On that occasion he was blessed with a deep spiritual experience, and recognized in Yogananda his own God-sent guru. He already belonged, however, to another spiritual work, and in fact served it in the capacity of president of one of its branch centers.

"What shall I do, sir?" he inquired. "How can I let all those people down?"

The Master's reply was simple and to the point: "Don't let sentiment rule you."

People naturally imagine that actions originate in their egos, and in sentiments born of ego-consciousness. In reality, however, all actions spring from currents of thought and energy that flow through the entire universe. Man is not what he seems.

The physical body, real as it appears, is only a holding-pattern of energy. The food one eats goes to the different body-parts, its molecules taking the form of fingernails, skin, muscles, and so on. They remain there only temporarily, however. Other molecules, their job finished, pass out of the body altogether.

The atoms of which our bodies are composed

don't belong to us, either. Who knows in how many former bodies, even in former universes, they once played a part?

Our personalities, again, are only foci for various aspects of Nature. A person's individuality might be compared to a light bulb, which seems to shine by its own light, but which in fact shines only by the electricity it receives from a power plant.

Love is not ours, when we express love. Nor is hatred ours, when we hate. Were human qualities not universally present in Nature, it would be no more possible for man to create them than for an artist to paint with nonexistent pigments.

Paramhansa Yogananda wrote in *Autobiography of a Yogi*, "Thoughts are universally and not individually rooted." Wise is that person who acts consciously as a channel for Nature in her higher, spiritual aspects. Such a person knows himself to be a part of Nature, and not "radically free," as certain philosophers like to insist.

Wisest, indeed, is he who looks always to God behind Nature as the real Doer. Such a person acts constantly from divine inspiration, and not from Nature, whether human or universal.

The true wealth of a great master lies in his perfect realization of God as the sole Reality. His disciples, however, often fall short of this vision. While intending to do him honor, they may turn the telescope of their perception the wrong way, their very praises reducing him, relatively speaking, to pygmy proportions. Constrained to concentrate on what they can see with their physical vision, they describe the master as great only in human terms,

27

not in terms of his divine omniscience.

Is love wonderful because Jesus loved? Rather, was not Jesus wonderful because he loved with such perfect, divine love?

And is salvation possible only through Jesus (or Krishna, or Buddha)? It is not these great masters, in their outward, human reality, who save humanity. It is the infinite Christ within, with which they are identified. They can bring salvation to mankind only because salvation is eternally the soul's destiny.

Jesus Christ himself said, "The things I do ye shall do also." Truth in its highest aspects is always impersonal. Religionists who insist on over-personalizing their beliefs might be accused even, in a sense, of blasphemy. Certainly that isn't their intention. Nevertheless, they belittle truth by trying to crop it, like a photograph, to fit their little frames of human understanding.

Jesus wisely began the Beatitudes with the words, "Blessed are the poor in spirit." The dispassion implied here forms the basis for the rest of the Beatitudes.

The perfect nonattachment taught also by Krishna in this passage of the Bhagavad Gita opens the door to ever-expanding vistas of truth beyond it. Nonattachment was the basis for his further discourse on the soul in its relation to God.

Jesus taught that the more we can empty ourselves and become as nothing before the Lord, the more perfectly we discover our entire existence in God. And Krishna, in this Gita passage, taught that the more we can separate ourselves from ego-involvement, the more perfectly we find ourselves immersed in God's love and joy.

These two teachings are not only similar: They are identical.

Thus, through the Bhagavad Gita, God has spoken to mankind.

Week 37

Basic Attitudes for Spiritual Development

Bible

The Beatitudes

This passage is from the Gospel of St. Matthew, Chapter 5, Verses 3-12:

"Blessed are the poor in spirit: for theirs is the kingdom of heaven.

"Blessed are they that mourn: for they shall be comforted.

"Blessed are the meek: for they shall inherit the earth.

"Blessed are they which do hunger and thirst after righteousness: for they shall be filled.

"Blessed are the merciful: for they shall obtain mercy.

"Blessed are the pure in heart: for they shall see God.

"Blessed are the peacemakers: for they shall be called the children of God.

"Blessed are they which are persecuted for righteousness' sake: for theirs is the kingdom of heaven.

"Blessed are ye, when men shall revile you, and persecute you, and shall say all manner of evil against you falsely, for my sake.

"Rejoice, and be exceeding glad: for great is your reward in heaven: for so persecuted they the prophets which were before you."

Commentary

The Beatitudes are verses in praise of divine attitudes. As no building can be erected on pillars of wet sand, even so without right attitude no spiritual progress can be made.

As we saw last week, the blessing promised in each of these verses sheds light on its accompanying virtue. Such light is needed. For language evolves over the centuries. Words not infrequently lose their original meaning, or acquire new nuances of meaning.

Some of the virtues listed in the Beatitudes no longer make sense, or else sound insipid to modern ears. Yet in fact all the Beatitudes offer profound spiritual teaching.

"Blessed are the poor in spirit: for theirs is the kingdom of heaven."

One may ask oneself, is this verse offering consolation for the losers of this world? In modern parlance, certainly, to be "poor in spirit" suggests at best an absence of fire. Stretching a point, one accepts that the expression refers to humility, but even with this interpretation the image that emerges is one of humility without warmth, or, alternatively, of submissiveness so self-abasing as to be almost abject.

Many Christians, indeed, attempting to imitate the humility of Jesus as they envision it from this Beatitude, make a practice of deferring to others, of gazing at people's knees instead of frankly into their eyes, and of smiling insipidly in reaction to every insult. This image of Jesus stands in broadest possible contrast to the dynamic Master who fearlessly drove the moneychangers out of the temple!

A submissive attitude toward life, as if in perpetual expectation of being misunderstood, is associated in many people's minds with saintliness. In fact, however, anecdotes from the lives of saints are rich with examples of a different kind of submission altogether: unflinching surrender, yes, but to God's will — and, at the same time, fearless opposition to error both in themselves and in those whom they are trying to raise spiritually.

Where is the gentle ramp up the mountainside to Perfection that might make the ascent easier for the faint-hearted? Heroic determination is a prerequisite for anyone who would deny the unceasing demands of his ego. Without great resolution, no one could dedicate himself wholeheartedly to God!

If the blessing promised to the "poor in spirit" is the kingdom of heaven, then we must look to courageous, not to defeatist, attitudes to explain what Jesus meant.

What Jesus intended here was that one should

rise above the ego-centric demands of human nature. The true disciple should empty himself and purify his heart's feelings until, like a polished chalice, he can reflect brightly in his very depths the sparkling nectar of God's grace.

To be "poor in spirit" means to be without delusive attachment of any kind. For only by perfect nonattachment, even to one's own self, can one enter the kingdom of God.

An example of such perfect nonattachment may be seen in the life of Paramhansa Yogananda. Praised once for his humility, he replied with beautiful simplicity, "How can there be humility, when there is no consciousness of self?" Humility itself, indeed, is transcended with the final conquest of ego.

How was it that Jesus, as perfectly ego-free as he was, could make such bold claims as, "I am the way, the truth, and the life"? Were any ordinary human being to make such a statement, would he not be thought unbalanced? It was with divine authority that Jesus spoke, for his consciousness was centered not in his humanity, but in the infinity of God.

"Blessed are they that mourn: for they shall be comforted."

The blessing promised here is not for human grief. Rather, it is a blessing that awaits every soul that longs deeply for God.

Here, once again, clarification can be found in the attendant blessing. "Comfort," in the human sense, is evanescent. Those who mourn do, no doubt, find consolation in time. This belated comfort, however, is no more lasting than the grief it assuages. Human emotions ever fluctuate. Satisfaction alternates ceaselessly with despair.

Were the comfort impermanent that Jesus promised to those who mourn, where would be the "blessedness" in it? At Jacob's well, he told the woman of Samaria, "Whosoever drinketh of this water shall thirst again: But whosoever drinketh of the water that I shall give him shall never thirst; but the water that I shall give him shall be in him a well of water springing up into everlasting life." (John 4:13-14) The promise that he made, then, to those who mourn was fragrant with divine, not with human, reassurance. He was saying that God eventually soothes the tears of every sincere devotee who longs for Him.

Many people, even among those who sincerely believe in the Lord, cannot bring themselves to believe that He really answers their prayers, or even hears them. Jesus in this Beatitude assures us that every sincere prayer is heard, and that it will be answered in time to our own deepest comfort and satisfaction.

Indeed, is not our very love for God assurance sufficient that the Lord *must* respond? Is He not the very love with which we pray?

A devotee once lamented to Paramhansa Yogananda, "I pray so earnestly that God come to me! Why is it that He hasn't come yet?"

With a blissful smile the master replied, "The Lord's delay is what makes it all the sweeter, when He does come!"

How often does the love one feels for another

34

human being go unrequited! Never does such disappointment befall the true devotee in his love for God. Sincere devotion is always requited. For God's love is forever ours. It is we, rather, who must at last requite His eternal love for us!

> *"Blessed are the meek: for they shall inherit the earth."*

Meekness, as the word is generally used today, seems a very colorless quality. It conjures up images in the mind of people weakly accepting the inevitable; images of timidity; of limp, long-suffering patience; or of simplicity so childish that it approaches simple-mindedness.

Do people in any of these categories ever "inherit the earth"? Quite the contrary! They are rarely found succeeding at anything. How is it possible, then, that these frail reeds will ever inherit the earth — except, perhaps, some minuscule portion of it from a deceased uncle?

"Meek" has, however, another dictionary meaning. It means *mild*. And "mild" can legitimately be understood in the sense of *harmonious* — in contrast to aggressive or self-imposing. "Harmonious," moreover, matches perfectly the blessing promised here by Jesus.

The harmonious do "inherit the earth." People who live in harmony with Nature and with divine law are those who receive the most back from life — far more so than the self-asserting, though often socially accepted, brigands who always seem to prefer to write their own rules.

Egotists break themselves on the rock walls of

Nature's opposition in their attempts to wrest from her the things they want. To people, however, who *attune* themselves humbly to Nature, she opens wide her doors, and showers them with limitless treasures.

Jesus, in promising the meek an earthly inheritance, obviously had no intention of strengthening their desire for earthly riches. He always tried to get people to forsake outward attachments. "Inheriting the earth," then, can only have had for him a deeply spiritual significance.

The inheritance he offered was a state of happy harmony with Nature, and also an ever-expanding harmony with God. The attainment of divine realization requires not that we repudiate Nature. Rather, the devotee must learn to live with Nature reciprocally, in ever-deepening, divine harmony.

"Blessed are they which do hunger and thirst after righteousness: for they shall be filled."

The word "righteousness," here, means righteousness in the eyes of God, not of others or of oneself. It means attunement with divine truth.

The more justified one is in one's own eyes — that is to say, with the smug confidence of egotism — the farther removed is he from true wisdom. Nor are things improved if he seeks justification in the eyes of the world. For before Truth, human opinion means nothing. Whatever is, simply *is*; opinions cannot change matters one way or another.

Hunger for moral rectitude, or for merely worldly wisdom, can never be assuaged permanently. To repeat Jesus' words to the woman of

Samaria, "Whosoever drinketh of this water shall thirst again." It is only hunger for divine truth that shall be satisfied at last, and forever.

"Blessed are the merciful: for they shall obtain mercy."

Mercy is of the heart, primarily, not of the head. It comes from empathy with others — that is to say, from feeling their joys and sorrows as one's own. The merciful are those who can feel themselves as if living also in others.

Such awareness comes increasingly with spiritual development. For the deepest reality of all men is God's presence within them. The more deeply we live centered in Him, the more clearly we discover His presence in all.

Jesus said, "Love thy neighbor as thyself." The original Greek says, "Love thy neighbor, he is like thee." Your neighbor is like you not only in the fact that he, like you, has a human form and personality, but more significantly in the fact that his soul-essence and yours are the same. In God, you and your neighbor are one.

Those people whose sympathies are broad, whenever they behold darkness in others, long to bring them light in order that they, too, might recognize their oneness with all life.

A person who does not love his fellowman will never win God's loving response. For God, who is Love itself, resides in the hearts of all. Mercy to all, on the other hand, even to those who hurt us, attracts the Lord's mercy in return.

Mercy means to view others in terms of *their*

good rather than of one's own.

To be merciful is to dispense kindness as if from above — obviously, not in a spirit of superiority, but rather with calmness, inner authority, and grace. One cannot help others if he allows himself to fall into their suffering, any more than one can help a drowning man by leaping into the water and drowning with him. To be merciful in the highest sense is to channel to others the awareness he feels of God's mercy within.

The more we serve consciously as channels for any aspect of God's grace, the more we ourselves receive of that special grace in the process.

Divine law ordains that we receive back from life, also, according to what we give out to it. Much is forgiven him, then, who forgives freely.

"Blessed are the pure in heart: for they shall see God."

Purity of heart is the fulfillment of nonattachment, which those people achieve who are "poor in spirit." Nonattachment requires mental affirmation and self-effort, at least in the beginning of the spiritual life. When nonattachment is perfected, it becomes purity of heart. Purity of heart is an effortless surrender of one's entire being into God's love.

Purity of heart is achieved when one's feelings have been purged of all that is foreign to one's true, spiritual nature.

Earth becomes dirt when it is tracked indoors on muddy boots. Out in the field, however, it is dignified with the name, *soil*. For the field is where it belongs. Impurities of the heart, similarly, in the sense implied in this Beatitude, are those desires and emotions which do not pertain to the soul. They need not refer to something filthy or evil. In a context of worldly involvement, an emotion may be quite right and wholesome: the perfectly normal desire, for example, for human love.

What makes an emotion impure from a higher, spiritual perspective, is that human feelings are foreign to the deepest nature of the soul.

Jesus says here that the pure in heart "shall see God." In John 1:18 we read a passage that seems to be in conflict with this promise: "No man hath seen God at any time." There is no contradiction, however. For it is never in our humanity that we can behold God, but in our souls.

To the devotee who loves God for Himself alone, the Lord reveals Himself at last, even to His deepest, most hidden mysteries.

"Blessed are the peacemakers: for they shall be called the children of God."

Peacemaking, in the sense Jesus meant here, involves more than the ability to persuade antagonists to cease fighting. The peacemaker is that devotee, rather, who lives in the consciousness of God's changeless inner peace.

Such a person, wherever he goes, emanates an aura of inner tranquillity. He may move among calm, spiritual people, or through dens of iniquity among people whose lives are in constant turmoil, but always he is at peace in himself. He wishes no harm to anyone; rather, he blesses all, self-styled enemies just as much as friends.

Peacemaking, in this divine sense, refers not to occasional deeds in the name of peace. Peacemaking is a constant, conscious emanation of inner peace toward the world around one.

Peace-emanating souls may rightly be spoken of as the children of God. They bring His peace to others. In this sense they are His emissaries.

Outward efforts to achieve peace on earth are ineffectual, because artificial. They fail to change the disharmonious attitudes that brought about conflict in the first place.

Those who live in God's peace, on the other hand, touch the souls of all they meet with a desire to drink at that eternal fountain.

"Blessed are they which are persecuted for righteousness' sake: for theirs is the kingdom of heaven."

Blessed indeed are they who, when faced with persecution, can stand firmly by the inner truths they know. For they demonstrate thereby, and at the same time deepen, their own perception that God and divine truth are the only things that matter in life.

Jesus wasn't speaking of persecution as a blessing in itself. Blessed are they, rather, who, even when persecuted, never compromise their ideals. By such divine steadfastness they prove themselves worthy at last to enter the kingdom of heaven.

* * * * * *

Such, then, is the inner meaning of the Beatitudes. They are a call to all sincere souls to dedicate themselves uncompromisingly to God. In no way do they justify the popular concept of a frail, almost cloud-like Jesus, expressed in that famous children's verse, "Gentle Jesus, meek and mild." The Master of Galilee is revealed in the Beatitudes, rather, as infinitely courageous in his dedication to Truth. Jesus in these verses challenges true seekers to become absorbed in God.

"Renounce ego!" he urges his followers, including all those today who would follow him to the heights of perfection.

"Yearn for the Lord from the very depths of your souls!

"Attune yourselves sensitively to divine truth. Never attempt vaingloriously to reshape the world in your own image, or according to your own desires.

"Live always by the highest principles. Follow the pathway to Truth. Spurn the fascinations of delusion!

"Expand your hearts' feelings, that you include in your compassion the well-being of all your earthly brothers and sisters.

"Purify your hearts; be totally open to God's will, and to His love.

"Remain inwardly unaffected by the storms of life. Seek always, with inner calmness, to bring divine peace on earth.

"In the face of death itself, finally, stand courageously by your eternal commitment to God alone!"

Thus, through the Holy Bible, God has spoken to mankind.

Bhagavad Gita

Blessedness Means Soul-Expansion

This passage is from the third Chapter, the 33rd and 34th Stanzas:

"All creatures live influenced by the qualities of Nature. Even the wise behave in accordance with Nature as it is manifested in them. Of what avail, then, is suppression?

"Attachment and repulsion to sense objects — both these are universally rooted. No one should accept their influence. For, verily, they are man's enemies."

Commentary

At first glance, these stanzas seem to be in conflict with each other. Is the first one saying that human nature can't be changed? The second, certainly, urges the importance of changing it. In fact, the first stanza only introduces the teaching in the second. It refers to the influences of cosmic Nature on human beings. In this context, the Gita proceeds in the second stanza to tell us how to alter our natural tendencies: not by suppressing them, nor yet by worrying about them or trying to reason our way out of them, but simply by changing our level of attunement with Nature, and with her universal influences.

Mankind, in contrast to the lower animals, has the heightened awareness to exercise some measure of free will. The more developed a person's awareness, the freer he finds himself to reject lower, negative influences, and to attract higher, spiritual ones. One cannot, however, improve himself if he repudiates all natural influences and tries to work out his salvation from the level of his little ego.

Thus, the statement that even the wise behave in accordance with Nature in no way implies that the will power of sages is shackled like everyone else's! Rather, this statement is meant to inspire hope. For it suggests to the struggling devotee that qualities that seem to him impossible to acquire will come, in time, to seem perfectly natural to him. He needs only to attune himself to higher influences. For nothing in his present nature defines him as he really is, in his soul.

The Bhagavad Gita is urging people to dissociate themselves from influences that are harmful to them, and open themselves to higher, beneficial ones. Every human weakness, it is saying, can be overcome. It also offers the right method for transcendence: not by trying to suppress human weaknesses, nor yet by attempting to think one's way out of them. Transcendence is achieved, rather, by soaring Godward in deep meditation, on beams of divine inspiration.

By suppression, man addresses his delusions only symptomatically, while ignoring their subtle cause. If boils should break out on the skin, what doctor worthy of the name would suggest curing them cosmetically? Physical ailments must be treated at their source.

This principle is true also for psychological ailments. If a person is afflicted with the compulsion to steal, will it cure him merely to tie his hands? Mental aberrations, too, must be corrected at their source.

Suppression means to refrain from indulging a desire while refusing to accept, or even to recognize, any viable alternative to it. With no outlet for emotional pressures, these only build up in the mind.

It is a different matter altogether to *resist* delusion. The second of these Gita stanzas makes it clear that resistance is essential. For a person's energy must be rechanneled upward, from self-destructive tendencies toward spiritually emancipating ones.

Nature influences us according to those levels of awareness at which we draw from her. The more sensitive a person is to her influences, the more selective also he can become in what he draws from her. The more uplifted his consciousness, the more elevating will be her influence on him. What we must do, then, to change ourselves, is work at changing our level of consciousness. It is of little avail to concentrate solely on correcting our faults, for these are only outward manifestations of the level of consciousness on which we live. Really to reform ourselves, we must meditate deeply and commune daily with God.

Let us resolve henceforth to fill our consciousness with divine inspiration. Transcendence, not worry, denial, and suppression, is the solution to all human problems. By attuning ourselves deeply to God — in Nature as well as beyond it — every human defect, every obstacle in our outer lives, can be overcome. There is nothing that can limit us forever. Eternally the path is open before us. The greatest of sinners can become a saint!

Thus, through the Bhagavad Gita, God has spoken to mankind.

How To Open the Conscious Mind to Superconsciousness

Bible

Become as a Child

This passage is from the Gospel of St. Mark, Chapter 10, Verses 13-15:

> *"And they brought young children to him, that he should touch them: and his disciples rebuked those that brought them.*
>
> *"But when Jesus saw it, he was much displeased, and said unto them, Suffer the little children to come unto me, and forbid them not: for of such is the kingdom of God.*
>
> *"Verily I say unto you, Whosoever shall not receive the kingdom of God as a little child, he shall not enter therein."*

Commentary

Jesus in these words is counseling a child*like* attitude, but not a child*ish* one.

There are two kinds of innocence. The one is born of ignorance; the other, of wisdom. Generally speaking, the innocence of children is of the first kind. Children have yet to experience evil. It is not that they have transcended evil. Life's battles, for them, have not yet been fought, nor its victories won. Most children, once they grow to adulthood and encounter the world's temptations, reveal themselves, in their inclinations, far from innocent!

Saints, on the other hand, have the innocence of wisdom. It is not that they are ignorant of the world's ways. Rather, they see that these ways are simply born of ignorance. Saints have discovered, hidden beneath all worldly turmoil, the eternal wonder and perfection of God's design.

Children ordinarily are both child*ish* and child*like*. In their self-involvement, in their emotions and tantrums, in their inability to relate to other people's realities, they are childish. And, in their wonderful openness and trust, they are childlike.

Children trust life because they have not yet been hurt by it. They have not yet seen their dreams shattered. They have yet to be disappointed or betrayed by other people.

The trust of saints, on the other hand, is not externalized. It is born not of the expectation of finding the world good, but of their realization that God is good. They are childlike in their openness and trust, not because they haven't known disillusionment, but because they are no longer susceptible to being disillusioned.

In fact, those who know God have no illusions left! Clear vision, however, does not leave them bitter. Quite the contrary, it fills them with joy! In their eyes, the realities of life are not ugly, for the deeper truths underlying them are eternally beautiful. The saints know everything in essence to be eternally good, because all things are manifestations of the divine.

Adults recognize it as their duty to raise their children to cope with reality. How is it, then, that they don't prepare youngsters from the very beginning for the bitter experiences of life? Whence, instead, the instinct most of us feel to protect children from disillusionment?

Is this instinct due only to our recognition that children, being small, need protection? Size, surely, is only a minor reason. A baby elephant, after all, is larger than an adult human being. Yet there is something about baby elephants, too, that awakens in everyone a special affection.

Surely, the reason lies in the nostalgia we feel on seeing the openness and trust in the eyes of the very young of every species. Don't we wish we, too, could believe once again in life's basic goodness? And might not our nostalgia arise from the fact that, deep within us, we know that it really *is* good? Cynical in our adult wisdom, we tell ourselves that goodness is only an illusion. The saints, however, by their lives show that it is evil, not goodness, that is the ultimate illusion.

This is why, the more deeply people's lives

become enmeshed in delusion, the more attached they become to evil. Delusion and evil are words for the same reality. So also are wisdom and goodness. Evil and sorrow, also, go together. So also do goodness and joy. Whoever first said of his experiences in life, "They left me sadder but wiser," had learned a degree of discrimination, but had not yet achieved wisdom.

There is another quality children and saints have in common. It is the ability to live fully, here and now. Children are much less inclined than adults to weigh everything in the balance, to compare present experiences with past ones, or with what others have experienced, or said, or thought. Children rarely weave complex webs of associated ideas around things. Life has not only spared most of them so far from disillusionment. It has also spared them from complexity.

The world teaches people very differently. In order to function rationally, they soon learn to weigh, to gaze skeptically, to compare this reality with that one, to judge every person, every situation. Surrounded by endless complexity, their own natures become complex also.

There is no need for complexity, however, in the spiritual world. Divine truths exist in another dimension altogether from that of the intellect, proud as it often is in its cleverness. Truth is basically simple. To enter the kingdom of God, we must suspend the normal processes of reasoning, and open ourselves to the clear flow of intuition.

The ego, as Paramhansa Yogananda remarked wryly, is pleased to find that it can grasp complexity.

Yet are not all men instinctively attracted to simple qualities: trust, openness, non-judgment? Indeed, we all know deeply within ourselves that it is *right* to live in simplicity, and not only because we wish life were easier than it is, or that people were more worthy of our trust. Indeed, do not all of us, occasionally in our lives — often quite unexpectedly — meet reminders of this deeper reality?

This nostalgia for simplicity is something basic to human nature. It is, the saints explain, a soul-longing for our lost home in God. For we are all God's children.

Worldly people, however, often challenge this teaching on practical grounds. "It's all very well," they say, "to be childlike and trusting before God in meditation! But what about when dealing with the 'market place' of this world, where people's entire aim is to get the better of you? Why, you'd lose your shirt!"

This perfectly reasonable objection is based on the common equation of innocence with ignorance, not with wisdom. Those who have achieved wisdom have had to deal first with lower realities. The saints may be visionaries, but they are not dreamers! Rather, in their daily lives they have often astonished worldly people by their practicality. One wonders why anyone would be surprised. It isn't as though airplane pilots forgot how to walk, or children how to crawl!

The difference between a saint in the market place and a worldly person is that the saint, there, doesn't assume a spirit of selfish competition. He deals honestly, fairly, intelligently, but he also considers the welfare of those with whom he must deal, and as conscientiously as he does his own. As a consequence, generally, those people find themselves dealing generously with him — no matter how piratical they may be when they bargain with other people.

The divine innocence of the wise can be acquired through deep meditation. In meditation one regains the experience of God, and, with that experience, perfect trust and faith in Him. The more one realizes that his true strength comes from within, and in no way depends on unstable outward circumstances, the more one finds his heart opening to the Lord. The openness achieved through meditation is much more profound than that of the child.

One who lives in God finds himself able once again to enjoy things for and in themselves. The freedom he recaptures is the bliss of his soul, lost to him through countless eons, but never forgotten in his inner Self. No longer does he feel the need to doubt, to weigh and compare everything before daring to accept it. Renouncing worldly sophistication, his heart becomes once more soft and trusting.

To rediscover these childlike traits in ourselves, we must develop simple, humble devotion to God. One enters the kingdom of God, so Jesus implies in this Bible passage, when one can become childlike in his faith in the Lord.

The key to becoming childlike is to hide no corner of our being from His scrutiny. We must learn to trust Him utterly, realizing that He alone can never disappoint us. We must learn not to weigh, compare, and evaluate whatever blessings we receive from Him, but to live fully, joyfully in Him, in the Eternal Now.

Thus, through the Holy Bible, God has spoken to mankind.

Bhagavad Gita

Overcoming the Carping Tendency

This passage is from the ninth Chapter, the first Stanza:

"The Blessed Lord said: 'To you, who are free from the carping spirit, I shall now reveal wisdom sublime. Grasping it with your mind, and perceiving it by intuitive realization, you shall escape the evils of delusion.'"

Commentary

To be free from the carping spirit means to return to the openness, trust, and wonder of a child. Paradoxically, it also means to achieve a state that is unusual for children, and all too unusual for adults: emotional maturity.

The road of life winds through a countryside of alternating victories and defeats, fulfillments and disappointments, flowery, green meadows and barren wastes. A sign of maturity is the ability to accept ups and downs with equanimity.

How few people are blessed with this ability! Young children typically respond to disappointment by weeping, or by throwing tantrums. Older children more often voice their frustration by complaining. And grownups, if ever they learn the futility of complaining, will often seek a kind of negative relief in criticism.

Many adults, resentful of a world that seems indifferent to their very existence, direct their fault-finding toward everything — their neighbors, the government, their place of work, the weather. It doesn't really matter what they find wrong with the universe. Their criticisms only serve to express their inner dissatisfaction.

People in whom the tendency to criticize is strong see themselves as the realists of this world. Nor are they mistaken, according to their own lights. The level of reality on which they live, however, is the well-traveled road, the unchallenging, because familiar. They lack that type of practicality which adventurous minds direct toward examining fresh possibilities.

Indeed, the very claim of carpers to realism, though based on common experience, falls short of the common sense to which they appeal in support of their criticisms. Their self-vaunted realism springs, rather, from wishing that things were other than they are. Carping, therefore, is really only a sign of immaturity.

Most people's lives are controlled by their desires. Because the world seldom caters to human expectations of it, the carping spirit may be found to some degree in nearly everybody. Thus, Krishna's compliment was high praise indeed.

The carping spirit is a manifestation of egotism. Implicit in its criticisms is the thought, "I could have done it better." It separates the critic from other people, and from the rest of the world. Spiritual progress, on the other hand, demands an expanding sense of unity with all life.

Typically, people with an exaggerated tendency to criticize defend themselves with such justifications as, "Well, *someone* has to play the devil's advocate!" In fact, however, their very concentration on the negative obstructs the constructive action that they claim they only want to promote.

It is true that there comes a time when critical evaluation becomes necessary. This time always comes later, however, not during the time of creative inspiration. Indeed, the most difficult part of the creative process is when creative ideas have reached the point where they need evaluation. The temptation, at this point, is to stray into a labyrinth of reasoning, thereby losing touch with the creative flow. At such times, one must exert great will power not to lose touch with his inner inspiration.

Great works of art, great inventions, great scientific discoveries — these never spring out of an exaggerated critical tendency. Nor do we find works such as these even coming from people who brood on the problems and difficulties in their work. Creative inspiration is not a product of the reasoning mind.

One sign of genius is a preference for concentrating on the search for solutions. Another is the practice of suspending reason and trying to "sense" one's answers. Creativity is not a rational act; it is an intuitive one.

The reasoning mind is naturally problem-oriented. It analyzes; it separates; it distinguishes objects and situations from one another. The reasoning faculty, when viewing any new reality, asks, "What makes this reality different?" Its comparisons are in order to distinguish things from one another. "Oranges are like tangerines, not like apples. On the other hand, oranges are larger than tangerines, and a little more sour."

Reason is problem-oriented because, instead of looking instinctively for the features that diverse phenomena have in common, it tends to view all things as unconnected events in space or time. It views problems, too, as unrelated to their inherent solutions. From each problem it considers, the reasoning mind tries to build bridges so as to relate it meaningfully to other events. Reason, to ascend the staircase of logical sequences, is forced to trudge laboriously from one step up to the next.

The superconscious mind, on the other hand, already sees everything as a unity. Its movement is a flow. It is solution-oriented, for, in its broader vision, it finds existing links between separate events and an infinity of other events, each of them suggesting countless creative possibilities.

The critical tendency belongs to the reasoning mind. Creative genius, on the other hand, belongs to the intuitive faculty. For creative work, the critical faculty must always be subordinated to the faculty of intuition.

True creativity constitutes a *relating to* reality, not merely an analysis of it. The negative, fault-finding tendency, on the other hand, constitutes a mental separation from reality. This is one explanation for why critics are generally mediocre as creative artists.

The carping spirit makes a person feel that he must weigh everything and judge it on its comparative merits. A person with this tendency steps back mentally from life's experiences, as though to dissociate himself from them. Burdened as he is with the illusion that the world awaits his judgment in breathless expectation (for human nature is inclined to project its attitudes onto the world around one), is it any wonder that the carper never really gets to enjoy life?

Devotees with a critical tendency, for the same reason, can never enter into the blissful flow of divine consciousness. Krishna, in this passage of the Gita, emphasizes Arjuna's freedom from the carping spirit. In so doing, he implies that openness, receptivity, and trust are fundamental attitudes for the devotee.

Elsewhere, again, Arjuna says to Krishna, "I am your disciple. Teach me." Only when the devotee can hold his understanding open to the flow of intuitive wisdom is he able to absorb all that his guru has to offer.

On the other hand, there is little that a master can

do to help that disciple who reasons incessantly, as though imagining himself a lawyer dealing with the opposition in court.

Krishna says here also that divine understanding cannot be separated from right, human attitudes. Thus, he tells Arjuna to grasp truth both with his mind and by intuitive perception. Our conscious attitudes, he is saying, need to be aligned with the flow of divine inspiration. Only when we open ourselves fully to that flow will grace descend into every level of our being, and liberate us from the evils of delusion.

Thus, through the Bhagavad Gita, God has spoken to mankind.

Religious Duty Varies with the Individual: How to Find One's Own Duty

Bible

Truth Is One; Many Are the Paths

This passage is from the Gospel of St. Luke, Chapter 9, Verses 49 and 50:

> *"And John answered and said, Master, we saw one casting out devils in thy name; and we forbad him, because he followeth not with us.*
> *"And Jesus said unto him, Forbid him not: for he that is not against us is for us."*

Commentary

Jesus in this story reveals a broad-mindedness that one doesn't often encounter among his followers.

It would be well for religionists everywhere to

understand the difference between dogma and dogmatism. A dogma is a definition of a spiritual truth. But dogmatism is the substitution of definitions for the truth itself. Dogmatism is an implicit denial of the need for any direct experience of spiritual realities.

Dogmas can be helpful. They may serve to clarify people's concepts. They may inspire them with deeper understanding. Dogmas, however, can also arrest further development. This they do if they tempt one to remain satisfied with whatever level of understanding he has reached so far in his spiritual growth. In this case, dogmas become dogmatism.

Bigotry is the mental calcification that develops when a person becomes so determinedly entrenched in his dogmatism that he erects protective walls around it to protect it from reasoned questioning. Dogmatism arrests further development, but bigotry is that mental and spiritual stagnation which ensues, once development ceases.

Dogmatism, and the fetid thought-forms spawned in its waters in the shape of bigotry, have nothing in common with the true spirit of religion. Both dogmatism and bigotry block the free-flowing river of soul-consciousness, and transform it, too, into a stagnant swamp.

True faith on the other hand, is an ever-widening wellspring of inspiration. It is like the joy that accompanies a new discovery: expansive, creative, all-embracing.

When Jesus counseled his disciples not to oppose those who were not in active conflict with his teachings, he was counseling an attitude of respect for other religious expressions.

Respect for other faiths and for other spiritual practices is a sign of spiritual maturity. Great masters invariably demonstrate appreciation for the religions of others. As a saint once said to Paramhansa Yogananda when Yogananda was a boy, "Isn't it true that the Lord's name sounds sweet from all lips, ignorant or wise?" It is the disciples of the masters, rather, who quarrel over differences in belief. And it is later generations of disciples who split theological hairs in their efforts to prove their own ways the best. Truth eludes them, for truth is one. It is the paths to it, only, that are varied.

To the extent that devotees deny other expressions of truth than their own, they deny the truth itself. They imagine by their dogmatism that they are demonstrating loyalty to their own teachings, whereas in fact they succeed in doing quite the opposite. They render a disservice to their own truth as well, when they seek to encase it within the narrow confines of dogmatism.

The true enemy of religion is not religious diversity. It is atheism. It is materialism.

Certainly the devotee should be loyal to his own spiritual path. The error so many devotees make is simply that they equate loyalty with narrow-mindedness, and dogma with dogmatism. Loyalty ought to broaden their perceptions, not shrink them.

A saint once said, "It is no doubt a good thing to be born into a religion, but it is a misfortune to die in one." What he meant was, "It is a good thing to be raised in religious teachings, but a pity to die entrenched in them, instead of having had one's consciousness expanded by them."

Jesus makes a statement elsewhere in the Bible that seems in direct contradiction to the tolerant reply he gave on this occasion. He tells the Pharisees, "He that is not with me is against me; and he that gathereth not with me scattereth abroad." (Matthew 12:30)

Countless Christians quote this second passage to support their claim that non-Christians, and even professed Christians whose interpretations of the Bible don't coincide with their own, are against Jesus. Few Christians seem even to have heard of Jesus' reply to the disciples in this week's passage. It is almost never quoted, certainly.

The fact is that Jesus, in saying, "He that is not with me is against me," was answering those who had accused him of casting out devils by the power of Satan. He was telling them that his was, instead, the power of God. He was simply saying, then, "Choose between God's power and the power of Satan." He was telling the Pharisees that, just as a demonic entity can be driven out only by its spiritual opposite, divine power, even so, anyone actively opposed to divine truth will have to be in league with that which opposes the truth: Satan. His words were not a condemnation of other ways of serving God, or of receiving divine inspiration.

It is a great blasphemy to defend one's own spiritual beliefs by denouncing those of others. Not only do people, by so doing, belittle truth itself: They also cheapen the dignity of their own potential relationship with God.

Disrespect for the insights and discoveries of

other cultures has prevented many a society from flourishing. If one's love for God is true, it can only be deepened by appreciation for the many ways in which divine love has found expression on earth. It is like the love a person feels for his own mother. Ought not his love to deepen his appreciation for motherly qualities in other women? Surely it is unthinkable that it inspire hatred, instead, for other women!

To an art lover, even primitive art can prove inspiring. For a true lover of God, similarly, the devotion even of primitive peoples can be inspiring. Certainly, unless it takes a decadent form, it is not something to be attacked.

We are all children of the same, one Father. It behooves us, if we sincerely love Him, to love and respect all others also in His name. Especially should we love and respect those who love Him, no matter what form their devotion to Him takes.

Thus, through the Holy Bible, God has spoken to mankind.

Bhagavad Gita

One's Duty Is Individual

This passage is from the third Chapter, the 35th Stanza:

"Trying, even if unsuccessfully, to fulfill one's own spiritual duty (dharma) is better than pursuing successfully the duties of others. Better even death in the pursuance of one's own duties. The pursuance of another's duties is fraught with (spiritual) danger."

Commentary

The word *dharma* means "duty." One's spiritual duty refers to those acts, specifically, which lead to soul-enlightenment.

Every Scripture enjoins general forms of behavior: to be kind; to be sincere; to speak the truth; to act in the interest of others and not only in one's own.

Certain types of behavior, besides, are mandated by a person's level of spiritual development. For the restless, service may be more beneficial than meditation. For the lazy, even ego-motivated action may be preferable to performing no action at all.

Certain acts, finally, are enjoined even more specifically, according to the tendencies a particular devotee needs to perfect or eliminate in himself.

In the above passage, the Bhagavad Gita is referring both to individual *dharma* and to the rules for people at various levels of spiritual development.

It was counsel according to individual *dharma* that Jesus Christ gave when, as we read at the end of the Gospel of St. John, he told Peter, "Feed my sheep." Peter then looked at John and said, "Lord, and what shall this man do?" Jesus answered, "If I will that he tarry till I come, what is that to thee? Follow thou me." (John 21:20-22)

It is important to realize that, apart from general moral maxims, there isn't any one path that is right for everyone. No particular set of practices, no particular system of beliefs, not even any particular religion is the best one for all. The more that universal truths become particularized, the more specialized, and hence limited in number, the group of people to whom they apply.

Certain monks are attracted to the cloistered life. Others are more inspired by a life of service. Those in the second group might feel spiritually suffocated in a cloister. And those in the first might find outward service disturbing to the inner calmness they are trying to develop. Who will say that either of these groups has made the better choice? Both are dedicated to pleasing God, perhaps both equally so. Their paths are different, but their goal is the same.

The same is true for the various world religions. Truth is one, even though the paths to it are diverse. Each individual must find that path which most inspires him in his own search for God. And each must consciously adopt that line of action — that *dharma*, in other words — which is most likely to free him personally from his spiritual limitations.

It is important when pondering this teaching to realize that a person's *dharma* is not necessarily determined by his talents. A devotee with a beautiful singing voice might be spiritually better off not becoming a professional singer. It depends on whether he finds divine inspiration in singing and can channel that inspiration to others, or whether there is a danger of his getting caught up in the delirium of popular acclaim.

It is never easy to make a critical choice of this nature for oneself. Usually it helps to seek advice from another, preferably one who is spiritually wise. Lacking a wise counselor, a good alternative would be to seek it from one who is removed from the problem emotionally.

To assume duties that are not one's own, spiritually, despite a possible aptitude for them, is dangerous not only because of the temptations they might pose to the ego. Delusion has countless ways of entering the mind and fanning the flames of desire.

The goal of right action is inner freedom, not bondage. Were one to pursue a plan of action that is not deeply rooted in his own nature, it might mean assuming to himself an entirely new set of tendencies, each one of which would have, eventually, to be worked out along with the pattern of unresolved tendencies that he already carries.

The humble devotee who pursues his own *dharma* with sincerity, even if he is not yet qualified to succeed in it, is far more securely on the path to liberation than one who seeks name and fame for the fleeting "success" of worldly applause. It is better to lose everything, even life itself, while doing one's spiritual duty than to take the "easy" path of success in a field that is not rightfully one's own.

As Emerson put it, "Imitation is suicide."

And as Shakespeare wrote:

"This above all: to thine own self be true,
And it must follow, as the night the day,
Thou canst not then be false to any man."

If the goal of right action is indeed freedom from attachments and desires, then success itself, ultimately, must be viewed in these terms. To succeed as a singer, spiritually speaking, means to relinquish attachment to the fruits of action, which in this case might be outward acclaim. To find spiritual success through singing, the singer should also seek to realize music as an aspect of the infinite "music" of Creation — the sound of *Aum,* as it is called in Sanskrit — by attuning himself inwardly to that sound.

Duty, in every case, is that which brings a person closer to God.

Thus, through the Bhagavad Gita, God has spoken to mankind.

Attuning Human Will to God's Infinite Will

Bible

Attunement to God's Will

This passage is from the Gospel of St. Matthew, Chapter 26, Verses 39-43:

"And he went a little farther, and fell on his face, and prayed, saying, O my Father, if it be possible, let this cup pass from me: nevertheless not as I will, but as thou wilt.

"And he cometh unto the disciples, and findeth them asleep, and saith unto Peter, What, could ye not watch with me one hour?

"Watch and pray, that ye enter not into temptation: the spirit indeed is willing, but the flesh is weak.

"He went away again the second time, and prayed, saying, O my Father, if this cup may not pass away from me, except I drink it, thy will be done.

"And he came and found them asleep again: for their eyes were heavy."

Commentary

This memorable scene occurs in the Garden of Gethsemane, on the night Jesus was betrayed. Jesus' firm will to accept the will of God, regardless of the consequences to himself, is an inspiring lesson for us all. The strength revealed by his obedience stands in poignant contrast to lack of it in his disciples.

The Master condoned their weakness, out of compassion for them. How, indeed, could he have scolded them on this night of all nights, except lovingly? At the same time, he was showing by his example what determination one must develop, to be worthy of knowing God.

Success on the spiritual path is not for the merely well-meaning. "The road to hell," it is said, "is paved with good intentions." Will power, never wishful thinking, is essential to success in any field. For will generates energy, and energy is what it takes to move mountains, whether with machinery or with the power of faith. "The greater the will," Paramhansa Yogananda used to say, "the greater the flow of energy."

Will power is a spiritual quality, essentially. Even worldly people with strong will power often have the potential for great spiritual development.

In normal everyday life, the will manifests itself less overwhelmingly, as willingness. Willingness was, above all, what Jesus demanded of his disciples. His very teaching said *Yes!* to life —

especially to a life lived in God. The magnetism of his presence was a constant affirmation of the *rightness* of living for God.

Willingness on the spiritual path means to say *Yes!* to God's will. By this attitude, one attunes himself ever more deeply to God's consciousness, thereby attracting unceasing blessings and joy.

It must be admitted, however, that the Lord tests His devotees! How else, indeed, could we perfect our willingness?

Often it seems as though, out of all possible choices, only that one indicated by God's will for us is *sure* to lead to disaster! In the end, the opposite invariably proves true: It is the other avenues, if taken, that lead to disaster. God's will leads infallibly not only to success, but to that fulfillment which we ourselves craved. His tests — sometimes administered, one can't help suspecting, with a touch of heavenly humor! — make our faith in Him eventually unshakable.

Because Jesus knew of his impending death, one might assume that his anguish in the garden of Gethsemane was a natural reaction to the approach of physical suffering. Yet he never showed himself attached to the body. The pains of his heart must have had a deeper cause. His sorrow, like his soul-consciousness, was universal, not personal. Weighing on his heart can only have been the remembrance of man's eternal rejection of God's love.

If at such an hour as that at Gethsemane Jesus could show compassion for others, as he did for his sleeping disciples, how much ought we to forget ourselves and be compassionate of others in the trivial hurts of our lives! And if, even at such an hour, he could show perfect willingness to accept God's will, how ready and willing ought we ourselves to be when we face the relatively petty trials of our own lives!

Habitual unwillingness is a common human condition, suggesting to the mind endless mountain ranges of problems in the discharge of the simplest duty. For just as willingness draws a constantly fresh supply of energy to the body, so also does unwillingness block that supply. "The greater the will, the greater the flow of energy." The corollary of that axiom is, "The greater the unwillingness, the feebler the flow of energy." We've all met people of such deep-seated unwillingness that, when merely answering the doorbell, they heave themselves groaning and sighing to their feet as if certain they were off to meet their martyrdom!

The greater the flow of energy to the brain, also, as a result of habitually willing oneself to think deeply or creatively, the greater one's mental capacity. This is, indeed, the simple secret of genius — an abundance of mental energy.

The weaker the energy-flow to the brain, on the other hand, the duller a person's awareness becomes. And this is the simple secret of stupidity.

Neither stupidity nor genius, however, can be achieved quickly. It takes time for energy to open up new channels in the brain, or for a lack thereof to close existing channels.

Here are a few simple rules for developing will power:

1. Never allow yourself to dwell on the no-

saying principle. Learn always to say *Yes* to life!

2. Look always for *solutions*, instead of concentrating too much on your problems.

3. Look for goodness in people; don't concentrate on their faults.

4. Train yourself to face life's challenges vigorously, always affirming, "I can!" — even when your mental habits cry out in protest, "Don't be ridiculous: How can you possibly?"

5. Set yourself specific tasks to accomplish — small ones at first, then increasingly challenging ones. Be sure to see each one through to completion.

6. Here is a technique that can help you to develop all-conquering will power: Concentrate at the point between the eyebrows, and around that point revolve the thought of increasingly powerful will power. Then affirm, with ever-greater conviction and magnetism, "My will is one with Thy will. United to Thine, my will can move mountains!"

When Jesus said, "The spirit indeed is willing, but the flesh is weak," he was referring to his disciples' spiritual debility in identifying themselves with their bodies. But he was also showing by his own example how all weakness can be overcome — never by accepting it, but by deepening one's attunement with the divine will. An attitude of willingness is the first, and forever essential, step in attuning our will to God's infinite will.

Thus, through the Holy Bible, God has spoken to mankind.

Bhagavad Gita

Signs of Divine Attunement

This passage is from the thirteenth Chapter, the
seventh to the eleventh Stanzas. It describes the nature of true wisdom.

"Humbleness, truthfulness, and harmlessness,
Patience and honor, reverence for the wise.
Purity, constancy, control of self,
Contempt for sense-delights, self-sacrifice,
Perception of the certainty of ill
In birth, old age, and frail mortality,
Disease, the ego's suffering, and sin;
Detachment, lightly holding thoughts of home,
Children, and wife — those ties which bind
      most men;
An ever-tranquil heart, heedless of good
Or adverse fortune, with the will upraised

> *To worship Me alone, unceasingly;*
> *Loving deep solitude, and shunning noise*
> *Of foolish crowds; calm focus on the Self*
> *Perceived within and in Infinity:*
> *These qualities reveal true Wisdom, Prince.*
> *All that is otherwise is ignorance!"*

Commentary

The above qualities are vital to the attainment of Self-realization. Though individual, they also express a unifying principle.

Humbleness means non-identification with the ego. This state can be achieved perfectly only in deep meditation.

Truthfulness, again, can be perfected only in meditation, with the realization that there is but one Reality, before which all else is illusory.

Harmlessness is perfected with the realization, again born of meditation, that all beings belong to one's own infinite Self.

Patience reflects in varying degrees the consciousness that time, space, and movement are delusions. This realization, too, is born in meditation.

Honor can be perfected only with the realization that there is but One Being whose satisfaction deserves courting: the Supreme Lord.

Reverence for the wise means openness to their guidance, and willing cooperation with it. It means to be open to wisdom itself. Wisdom is theirs alone who meditate deeply. For it differs from knowledge. Knowledge is of the intellect, whereas wisdom is of the soul.

To the sincere truth seeker, God sends one of His awakened sons to guide him out of delusion. The master specifically appointed to this task is known as the *guru*. The disciple, by loving service to the guru, receives through him the gift of wisdom. This is what is meant in the Bible in the passage, "But as many as received him, to them gave he power to become the sons of God." (John 1:12)

Service to the guru is primarily an inner act. It means offering up to him, in deep meditation, all one's worldly thoughts and desires. It means constantly holding one's consciousness open to him for correction and inspiration. Above all, it means attuning oneself inwardly to his consciousness of God.

Purity arises naturally in the mind, the more one's thoughts and feelings become cleansed in crystal streams of ecstasy.

Steadfastness develops spontaneously, the more one's mental rhythms change from fixation on temporal pleasures to absorption in eternal realities.

Self-control, like all divine qualities, has to be worked on consciously. At the same time, progress in self-control ceases to demand strenuous effort the more one identifies himself with the soul, removing his attention from the world of the senses and the ego.

Contempt for sense-delights — that is to say, indifference to them — comes not so much with straining to acquire mental detachment from them as with the realization of a higher bliss, through inner communion with God.

Self-sacrifice springs from the absence of self-interest. It doesn't mean self-abnegation. Self-sacrifice

might be better understood as joyous self-*offering*.
This impulse arises naturally in the mind, once one
realizes himself as the underlying Self of all.

Perception of the evils inherent in mortal life is possible, in the deepest sense, only when, in meditation,
one dives beneath the waves of duality — of pleasure and pain, success and failure, hope and dread
— which continually rise and fall on the surface of
life. In deep meditation, the yogi realizes how limited human existence is compared to the vastness of
God's ocean. For the soul, pleasure is not essentially
different from pain. Both are simply affirmations of
limitation.

Detachment from outer concerns is possible, in the
deepest sense, only by attachment to the infinitely
greater joy of divine communion. Non-identification with family, home, and possessions comes naturally to one who knows to the depths of his being
that he belongs to God alone.

An ever-tranquil heart comes naturally when the
waves of likes and dislikes become stilled forever in
the calmness of divine perception.

Unswerving devotion to God alone is not possible in
ego-consciousness, but is the fruit of deep communion with God.

Love of solitude deepens, the more forcefully one
feels himself called within by God. For the true
devotee, indeed, worldly company holds no attrac-
tion.

Concentration on the inner Self, finally, is a fitting
definition of wisdom. Any other attitude, as the Gita
states here, is ignorance. A person may be completely illiterate. He may possess no worldly talents

whatever. If, at the same time, he is blessed with the realization of who and what he really is in his soul, his wisdom is far greater than all the learning and experience of the worldly-wise.

One condition unites all the above qualities: It is the state known as Self-realization. Together, these qualities are perfected only with the attainment of divine union.

Most people on the spiritual path make the mistake of thinking that right spiritual attitude can only be achieved by mental affirmation. These attitudes, however, can be perfected only by the daily practice of deep, inner communion with God. For it is divine grace alone, finally, that lifts the devotee out of delusion and into Divine Perfection

Thus, through the Bhagavad Gita, God has spoken to mankind.

The Two Sides of Renunciation, and How They Affect Every Devotee

Bible

The Need for Austerity

This passage is from the Gospel of St. Matthew, Chapter 10, Verses 34-39:

> *"Think not that I am come to send peace on earth: I came not to send peace, but a sword.*
>
> *"For I am come to set a man at variance against his father, and the daughter against her mother, and the daughter in law against her mother in law.*
>
> *"And a man's foes shall be they of his own household.*
>
> *"He that loveth father or mother more than me is not worthy of me: and he that loveth son or daughter more than me is not worthy of me.*
>
> *"And he that taketh not his cross, and fol-*

loweth after me, is not worthy of me.
"He that findeth his life shall lose it: and he
that loseth his life for my sake shall find it."

Commentary

In this important passage we see Jesus placing strong emphasis on austerity. He doesn't equate austerity with harshness, but with unswerving dedication to God and to the divine search.

It would be easy to take Jesus' words here literally, as bellicose. If, however, we consider them in the broader context of his life mission, we quickly see that he was speaking thus only to light a fire of divine courage in the hearts of devotees. In saying that he had come not to bring peace but a sword, he wasn't being a firebrand revolutionary. (This, in fact, is how certain modern writers have described him!) He meant "sword" symbolically, referring to the determination one needs to find God. *Sword*, in this sense, is an apt metaphor, for the devotee must be prepared to do battle in his confrontations with delusion.

Sword is also a reference to the keen-edged power of discrimination, which severs the bonds of outward attachments. Jesus' reference to setting a son against his father, and a daughter against her mother, was not an attempt to destroy the family unit. It was simply an effort to inspire his disciples to sever their emotional attachment to everything and everyone.

The power of cosmic delusion is conscious, and tries to keep all men bound to matter. The satanic force holds before our imagination attractive scenes of family and home life. It suggests to the mind the pleasant normality that worldly people share: "Others live this way," it says. "Why do *you* presume to be different?"

Indeed, even if one's relatives are worldly, one should always love them in God. A relative who shares one's love for God is, moreover, a great blessing. But if the only thing one's close relatives want is to wrap him in familial warmth, he then faces a choice between accepting the ego-identity they represent, or expanding his sense of kinship to embrace all mankind.

Jesus himself made it clear that family and other relationships, as such, should be respected. Anyone, however, who opposes the devotee in his search for God must be met with firm resistance. This does not mean that one shouldn't inwardly bless everyone, friend and self-defined foe alike.

"He that taketh not his cross, and followeth after me, is not worthy of me." The spiritual path is not for "armchair" devotees. It is for spiritual warriors. The path is for those who would embrace death itself, rather than abandon their divine search.

"He that findeth his life shall lose it: and he that loseth his life for my sake shall find it." The devotee, in deep inner communion with God, attains a state where he realizes that the next step is to offer his very ego into the ocean of bliss. Thus alone is it possible to attain union with God. It is a great challenge. The entire spiritual path is a training for this moment: all the service, the devotion, the discrimination, the humility, the chanting, the meditation. Whosoever draws back from this final offering makes the choice to maintain his separateness from God. Losing courage even at this late stage on the path, he loses the opportunity to attain infinite life — at least for this lifetime.

The destiny of the soul lies in realizing the truth of Jesus' words, "I and my Father are One."

Thus, through the Holy Bible, God has spoken to mankind.

Bhagavad Gita

Life Is a Dream

This passage is from the fourteenth Chapter, the 24th and 25th Stanzas. In these Stanzas Krishna describes the enlightened sage:

> "Unaffected by outward joys and sorrows, or by praise and blame; secure in his divine nature; regarding with equal gaze a clod of mud, a stone, and a bar of gold; impartial toward all experiences, whether pleasant or unpleasant; firm-minded; untouched by either praise or blame; treating everyone alike whether friend or foe; free from the delusion that, in anything he does, he is the doer: Such an one has transcended Nature's triune qualities."

Commentary

In this passage we find expressed the positive side of austerity. Austerity, as presented here, doesn't mean fanaticism or exaggerated self-discipline. Rather, it signifies the calm realization that this universe is only a dream, and that nothing matters except God's love and the eternal joy of loving Him.

Strenuous effort is required, certainly — especially in the early stages of the spiritual life — to reject all delusive attachments and desires. The devotee can avoid discouragement by reflecting on the bright side of renunciation: the soul's eventual freedom in God. In that divine state, he should remind himself, the soul will be untouched by delusion of any kind. Devastating storms of emotion may rage around him: He will remain ever at the storm's center: blissful, self-possessed.

Renunciation without the thought of its higher purpose may set a person in conflict with himself. Or, again, one who embraces renunciation for its own sake may sink into that smug self-righteousness which is more or less the only reward people get who follow the spiritual path joylessly.

When a businessman reinvests some of his profits instead of spending them, it is in the hope of increasing his prosperity. And when a person refrains from replying cuttingly to a verbal assault from a friend, it is to preserve their friendship. Mature human beings realize that worthwhile goals can be achieved only if they invest energy toward them instead of squandering it.

The same is true on the spiritual path. Renunciation represents an investment: the lesser interest in exchange for the greatest of all possible gains.

People often remonstrate, "When you go off and meditate, you are only avoiding life!" This charge can be answered with a simple question: Do they themselves reproach high school graduates for going on to college, instead of immediately seeking jobs? Certainly not! They know that a higher education will help them to find better jobs later on. The same is true for the spiritual search.

The devotee who meditates daily gains increasing mental clarity. In this sense, indeed, he finds immediate benefits from meditation, as well as long-term ones. His increasing inner clarity enables him to cope efficiently with the most mundane problems.

Thus, through the Bhagavad Gita, God has spoken to mankind.

The Supreme Secret of Success

Bible

First Things First

This passage is from the Gospel of St. Matthew, Chapter 6, Verse 33:

"Seek ye first the kingdom of God, and his righteousness; and all these things shall be added unto you."

Commentary

Worldly people think first in terms of attaining outward security: money, success, comfort, fame. After that — who knows? Maybe God too, someday. Erring in their priorities, they find their goals receding ever before them like tendrils of mist on the wind.

Life is like a puppet constructed of pieces of wood and held together by a string. The string of this type of puppet is tied in a knot at the top of the head. If one picks the puppet up at any place but at that knot, it hangs shapelessly. But if one picks it up by the knot, the pieces fall into place and assume the shape of a human being.

With us, similarly, when the focus of our attention is God, everything in our lives falls naturally into place. Inner contentment is ours, and outer harmony as well. Success no longer flees mockingly before us. Every worthwhile goal becomes attainable, if not easily, at least certainly.

To live by faith, as Jesus suggests in this passage, is the most practical thing a person can do. Most people, in the name of being "practical," put God last in their lives. They wonder, then, why nothing ever goes quite right for them. The devotee, on the other hand, and also in the name of practicality (since his dedication is to truth), puts God first in his life. He attains fulfillment on every level of his existence. To his continued amazement, he finds himself protected in adversity, saved from the jaws of disaster, and guided in every crisis in ways that often leave his worldly friends shaking their heads in wonder and muttering, "Fools' luck!"

The most important thing for every human being, whatever his other goals in life, is to cultivate faith in God.

Faith is far more than belief. It is the *consciousness* of God's presence within.

To become a good artist, a person must cultivate the *consciousness* of an artist. To become a successful businessman, one must cultivate the proper *consciousness* for success in business. One cannot become a good artist if he thinks of his work primarily as a business venture. Nor can one become a good businessman if he subordinates investment and profit to esthetic considerations.

In India, the religious attitude of immersing oneself in the thought of God is expressed by the word, *bhav*. This word has a double meaning. It is the mental image one holds of God; it is also the image one holds of himself in his relation to God.

Bhav concerns the devotional attitude of the devotee who seeks God above all for His love. The sincere devotee is not concerned with correctly defining God. How, indeed, could the human mind ever comprehend Him? It is not with our thoughts that we can reach Him, Who dwells beyond the farthest boundaries of thought. What we must do instead is visualize Him in a way that will inspire us to love Him deeply.

The variety of incentives to which people are capable of responding is endless. A certain devotee, greatly attracted to food, received a joyful boost in his devotion when he read once in a book: "The experience of God can come also in the form of a thousand delicious tastes all crushed into one"!

Devotees may be inspired to love God by visualizing Him in a human form: as their Heavenly Father, for example, or as their all-compassionate Divine Mother. Again, they may visualize Him as manifested through one of the great masters who are sent to earth by God as messengers of His love. In visualizing a master's kind eyes and loving smile, it is often easier to visualize the infinite love of God.

Again, one may feel more devotionally inspired

if he visualizes the Lord as infinite — or, again, as dwelling as an invisible Presence in every tree, every flower, in the mountains, and in all creatures.

Visualizations are helpful for the devotion they inspire in the devotee. One should not lose sight, however, of the fact that God is infinitely beyond man's ability to visualize Him. This does not mean that God is not *also* our visualizations of Him. God is in everything. In a sense, He *is* everything. He responds consciously according to whatever form we visualize lovingly. If we look to Him in Nature, He responds through Nature. If we look to Him as our Divine Mother, He responds to us with Motherly love. If we look to Him as our Father, He responds as a Father, with deep wisdom and understanding. His response depends on the deepest needs of our own hearts.

Through great masters, and to a lesser degree through saints and the angels in heaven, God responds in a special way. For it is their mission, as conscious emissaries of His love, to help those who long for spiritual understanding. Visualizing God in any form is a means of activating His response. Through awakened or highly advanced souls, however, He is already working for the salvation of mankind.

The best practice is to call to God in whatever aspect one finds most inspiring, but then also to invoke the help of a great master, saint, or angel in order that, by attuning oneself to their love for God, one come to understand pure love, and thereby deepen one's own love for Him.

Focus your mind one-pointedly on whatever

aspect of God most inspires you. Don't roam about in your mind like a bee that can't decide from which flower it wants to sip honey. The corollary to your visualization of God is how you see yourself in relationship to Him. If you think of God as your Divine Mother, develop the trusting attitude of a child. If you think of God as your Heavenly Father, see yourself in the role of loving son, or of devoted daughter.

One's *bhav* becomes increasingly refined, the farther he advances spiritually. The devotee who at first loves God as his Divine Mother, and visualizes Her in a human form, comes in time to perceive Her everywhere: formless, infinite, omnipresent, yet forever motherly.

Bhav is more a matter of loving God than of receiving blessings from Him. Like the knotted string at the top of the puppet's head, when one's heart and mind are drawn upward in focus on God alone, one is capable of receiving His response, of communing with Him, and of being led by Him toward final enlightenment. The more one immerses himself in the divine consciousness, the more he finds all his outer needs also, as Jesus said, being fulfilled.

There is, furthermore, a physical method for practicing this precept. If one keeps his mind focused always at the point between the eyebrows (the seat of spiritual vision in the body), he experiences harmony not only in his relationship with God, but in the body as well. As Jesus said, "If thine eye be single, thy whole body shall be full of light." (Matthew 6:22) Because one's experiences in life are reflections of his own consciousness, everything outward in one's life becomes harmonized as well, once one achieves inner harmony.

Jesus urges all who have sought fulfillment unsuccessfully through outward channels to seek it where alone it can be found: in the Lord.

Thus, through the Holy Bible, God has spoken to mankind.

Bhagavad Gita

Secrets of Worship

This passage is excerpted from the ninth Chapter, the 25th Stanza:

"Those who worship lesser gods go to their gods ... but those who worship Me come to Me."

Commentary

This stanza, in its complete form, contrasts various levels of experience in an after-death state in the astral world with the state of final union with God. The great truth expressed by this stanza, however, can be applied equally well to the contrast between divine union and the attainment of worldly goals.

For the average person, material ends are his "gods." He worships them with a devotion that would win great spiritual rewards, were his efforts only directed toward divine attainment!

Worship might be defined thus: *to be absorbed in the contemplation of some great good, whether real or imaginary.* Worship is not the mere performance of outward religious rites: It is a matter of inner *attitude.* Rituals are meaningless without devotion. A man might go to church regularly, but if inwardly he is absorbed in dreaming of some profitable business venture, then in fact what he is worshiping is money. Hence the Biblical commandment, "Thou shalt have no other gods before Me."

The direction of a person's desires determines the direction his life will take, too, and indicates what he will eventually become. "Those who worship lesser gods go to their gods." Absorption in the thought of any goal whatsoever, in the conviction that it is a great good, draws a person to that sphere of existence. One comes to reflect its realities, however illusory, in his consciousness. And he attracts those people, situations, and opportunities which will reinforce his convictions.

If a person lives only to revenge himself on his enemies, his obsession for revenge will remain with him long after he has, as he thinks, "evened things" with them. Others will be attracted to him who harbor similar desires for revenge. Thus, reinforcing one another in their bitterness, they may all come in time to look upon vengeance as almost a sacred principle.

For a person who wants to become a great artist, and who absorbs himself in the "worship" of art as a great good, art becomes his god. He will, accordingly, "go to that god," as his life becomes progressively centered in art alone. The friends he attracts will be artists. In time, he may find it difficult even to imagine, except possibly in caricature, any other sphere of activity.

It is interesting to see how quickly newcomers to a city manage to encounter their own kind. Within hours, thieves manage to meet other thieves; drunkards, to find other drunkards. Businessmen are soon mixing with other businessmen; artists, with fellow artists. And devotees very soon meet others who love God. Long-term residents may be unaware of how many types of humanity jostle their way through their city's streets.

Does the need to absorb oneself in whatever one does, if one would become good at it, mean that one will "go to that god" instead of to the Supreme Lord? Is it necessary, in other words, for the devotee to avoid being good at anything, so as not to divert his devotion away from God? This is an example of the kind of confusion into which people can stray when they remove spiritual teaching from the practical experience of their own lives.

The fact is, to become good at anything is a help, not a hindrance, in anything else one attempts to accomplish. God-communion is not their last chance at glory for the failures of this world!

The important thing is not to *worship* whatever one does in life — that is, not to look upon it as a supreme good. One should view it instead as simply something that requires doing. The best work in any case is that which is done in a consciousness of inner freedom, in the thought of God, and for the glory of God — offering, as the Gita teaches, the fruit of one's actions to the Lord. Such a person not only finds God, but, while seeking Him, discovers that success in any other field comes to him as well.

Hence the importance of *bhav*, the attitude the devotee holds in his relationship with the Lord. "Those who worship Me come to Me." To worship God means to approach Him with an attitude of love, of dedication and self-offering, of total absorption in the contemplation of Him in deep inner communion. Those whose lives thus revolve around their desire for God will surely come to Him. Such is the Lord's promise.

Thus, through the Bhagavad Gita, God has spoken to mankind.

Part VII

How To Pray
Effectively

God: Form or Formless? How Best To Pray to Him, and Why

Bible

"Our Father"

This passage is from the Gospel of St. Matthew, Chapter 6, Verses 7-13:

"But when ye pray, use not vain repetitions, as the heathen do: for they think that they shall be heard for their much speaking.

"Be not ye therefore like unto them: for your Father knoweth what things ye have need of, before ye ask him.

"After this manner therefore pray ye: Our Father which art in heaven, Hallowed be thy name.

"Thy kingdom come. Thy will be done in earth, as it is in heaven.

"Give us this day our daily bread.
"And forgive us our debts, as we forgive our
debtors.
"And lead us not into temptation, but deliver
us from evil: For thine is the kingdom, and the
power, and the glory, for ever. Amen."

Commentary

The Maharani of the state of Cooch Behar, in India, once asked her family priest, "Why do you make such a clamor of bells, conch shells, and shouting while conducting worship services in the temple?"

"Well, you see, your Highness," explained the priest, who was somewhat out of his depth in theological matters, "God is deaf. How can we attract His attention, if we don't make a lot of noise?"

The same priest once approached the Maharani for a temple donation. He required, he said, the finest grade of whiskey, naming a brand which, he explained, God especially liked. "It's for pouring libations," he told her, "during worship services."

"Other priests use plain water," replied the Maharani. "What you really want, it seems to me, is libations for the 'temple' of your body, so you can offer them into the 'altar' of your own stomach!"

How could anyone imagine that the Lord can hear our prayers only if we shout them loudly? — that He notices worshipers only if they make exaggerated gestures? — or that He is pleased with them only when they flatter Him, to the fragrant accompaniment of burning incense? Jesus, like all the masters of India, ridiculed the idea of addressing God as though He were capable of perceiving only through the five senses, like a human being. God is without form. He is infinite. As Jesus told the woman of Samaria, "God is a Spirit."

The Lord hears us, because He resides always in our hearts. He hears us, because He already *is* the words with which we pray. To pray effectively, Jesus said, we must approach Him as our own nearest and dearest.

In this context, the most important words in the Lord's Prayer are those first two: "Our Father." Man finds it difficult to direct love toward something he can't visualize. God, though infinite, is not limited even by His infinity! The Lord, out of Whose vast consciousness everything in existence was manifested, has become also personal in human beings, though few human beings are aware of His indwelling presence. As He manifests Himself also in things finite, so He can respond to us consciously in whatever form we hold dear.

Everything, in a sense, tells us something of His presence. The mighty oak speaks to us of His strength and firmness. The gentle rain whispers to us of His mercy and grace. The bounding streams sing to us that truth is ever-flowing, and cannot be imprisoned in little cups of dogmatism. The ocean offers sermons on God's vastness. The smiling flowers tell us tales of His supernal beauty. The rainbows send us radiant messages of hope.

Human fathers, if they are just and kind to their children, afford glimpses of God's limitless justice, kindness, and wisdom. Mothers, if they are selfless and compassionate, afford glimpses of God's unconditional compassion and love.

We can love God as our Father, and offer ourselves up to Him with perfect trust in His wisdom. We can love God also as our Mother, as our Friend — even as our Beloved. For God is all of these, and infinitely more besides. The important thing is to approach Him with deep love and trust. For He is nearer than our own nearest thoughts. As Jesus put it, "Your Father knoweth what things ye have need of, before ye ask him."

To pray effectively, we must think of God as a listening, loving, interested, ever-accepting Presence. We must have confidence in Him, that He will always take care of us if only we approach Him with deep love. He is already our Father, if that is the relationship with Him that we want. He is already our Mother, if that is the relationship that we hold most dear. Always, and in whatever way we worship Him, He is already our very own.

The most important aspect of prayer, and that which makes it possible even to perform great miracles, is unconditional, ever-trusting love for God.

Thus, through the Holy Bible, God has spoken to mankind.

Bhagavad Gita

God — Personal or Impersonal?

This passage is from the twelfth Chapter, the first, second, and fifth Stanzas:

"Arjuna said, 'Those who, ever steadfast, worship Thee as devotees, and those who contemplate Thee as the immortal, unmanifested Spirit — which group is the better versed in yoga?'
The blessed Lord replied: 'Those who, fixing their minds on Me, adore Me, ever united to me through supreme devotion, are in My eyes the perfect knowers of yoga....
"'Those whose strict aim is union with the Unmanifested choose a more difficult way; arduous for embodied beings is the path of dedication to the Absolute.'"

Commentary

Arjuna asks here whether it is better to worship God with form, or to dwell on the more austere thought of Him as impersonal and formless.

It is important when studying this passage to realize that Arjuna poses his question right after experiencing God in His formless state. What Arjuna asks is not which reality is the higher, but rather which mode of worship is preferable for the devotee, even assuming that one aspires to reach that highest state.

For human beings, Sri Krishna answers, living as they do in physical bodies, it is difficult to feel devotion to formlessness. To contemplate God as an Infinite Void could lead them into spiritual vagueness.

Even when undertaking worldly projects, if a person hasn't a clear idea of what it is he wants to accomplish, he won't find it easy to give direction to his energies. His ideas may change in time, as he gains experience. At every stage of his progress, however, he needs a clear sense of purpose. Otherwise he will find himself merely drifting.

It is not impossible to attain God by worshiping Him as the Unmanifested. The path of wisdom, or *Gyana Yoga*, however, is not what most philosophically minded seekers imagine it to be. It is not a path for intellectuals who want exact, carefully worded definitions. And it is certainly not a path for fuzzy-minded, so-called intellectuals whose sense of truth is satisfied with vague words such as "Absolute," or "Unqualifiable." *Gyana Yoga* begins and ends with the task of demolishing the sense of "I" and merging it into the divine consciousness.

In pure *Gyana Yoga* there can be no analysis of Truth, for the simple reason that the intellect itself doesn't belong to Absolute Reality. Nor is it really consonant with *Gyana Yoga* to practice yoga exercises, or yoga breathing and meditation techniques. One who refuses to recognize God in form cannot conscientiously recognize even his own physical form. Thus, the *gyana yogi* is enjoined to live in the thought that nothing, not even his own mind, intellect, ego, and feelings, has any reality at all.

To live in this state of awareness is difficult for most people, if not quite impossible. As Krishna states elsewhere in the Bhagavad Gita, moreover, the yoga meditation techniques, which help to calm the body and mind and to develop concentration, are a great aid on the spiritual path. Affirmations of abstract truth, without practical assistance from scientific spiritual methods, can take only a very few rare souls to the infinite shores. Even those truth seekers who succeed at last in soaring spiritually deprive themselves of the subtle assistance that yoga practices would provide them. To break the bonds of attachment to body and senses by mental effort alone is a lengthy process indeed.

Most self-styled *gyana yogis* fall far short of the *gyanic* ideal. They conceal beneath a pretense of sagacity the fact that they lack heart quality. Even the *gyana yogi* needs to awaken love in his heart. Otherwise he will never succeed in his spiritual quest.

Best, for mankind, is the path of devotion to God, of visualizing Him as endowed with form. Best is it for one to accept his humanity as his starting point.

It is best, in other words, to recognize and deal with one's own present realities if he would rise to increasingly subtle heights of understanding. Devotional love, combined with the practice of scientific yoga techniques, is the surest and fastest path to God. As Sri Krishna says elsewhere in the Bhagavad Gita: "Arjuna, be thou a yogi!"

One who worships the Infinite in a finite expression should always be aware that God cannot be confined in a form. Behind any form that one visualizes, one should visualize the consciousness of infinity. For if we want to avoid the pitfall of dogmatism, we must desire that our understanding ever expand.

Jesus Christ began the Lord's Prayer with the words, "Our Father." Hence its common name, the "Our Father." That word, *our*, is a reminder that God is the Father of *all* His human children, and not the special property of any one worshiper or congregation of worshipers. It would be foolish to say that one's own way of worshiping God, or that any definition of God formulated in his religion, is the last word in divine truth. God, though loved and worshiped by human beings in personal terms that they can visualize, *is*, after all, far more than anything they can ever visualize. As a certain Indian saint put it, when speaking once of the Spirit as inconceivable by human minds: "It is, and It isn't; and neither is It, nor is It not"! The Lord, in other words, cannot be captured mentally. It is we who must allow ourselves to be captured by Him! And yet, we can make Him forever the Prisoner of our hearts' love.

Thus, through the Bhagavad Gita, God has spoken to mankind.

The Lord's Prayer: How To Harmonize Human with Divine Nature

Bible

The Lord's Prayer

This passage is from the Gospel of St. Matthew, Chapter 6, Verses 7-15:

"But when ye pray, use not vain repetitions, as the heathen do: for they think that they shall be heard for their much speaking.

"Be not ye therefore like unto them: for your Father knoweth what things ye have need of, before ye ask him.

"After this manner therefore pray ye: Our Father which art in heaven, Hallowed be thy name.

"Thy kingdom come. Thy will be done in earth, as it is in heaven.

"Give us this day our daily bread.

"And forgive us our debts, as we forgive our debtors.

"And lead us not into temptation, but deliver us from evil: For thine is the kingdom, and the power, and the glory, for ever. Amen.

"For if ye forgive men their trespasses, your heavenly Father will also forgive you:

"But if ye forgive not men their trespasses, neither will your Father forgive your trespasses."

Commentary

There is no need, Jesus says, to "nag" God with endless entreaties. It is enough to pray with the simple confidence of a child addressing his father.

Many people pray, instead, as though they didn't really believe God was listening to them. They roam here and there in their minds, vaguely tossing half-finished thoughts into a cavernous void. This is, in fact, the special advantage of formal prayer: At least it helps one to keep his prayers from becoming a mere stream of consciousness!

With the Lord's Prayer, Jesus offers a perfect prayer-formula. At the same time, his prayer avoids the disadvantage of most formal prayers. (How often we've heard them: dry, solemn petitions, delivered as if to impress an almighty, but indifferent, Emperor.) How different is the Lord's Prayer! It is a loving statement of openness to God, of perfect trust in Him.

It is also much more. To understand it deeply, we must reflect that Jesus' mission on earth was to help souls to rediscover their lost sonship with the

Father. In this context it is clear that this central prayer of the Christian faith is more a guide to man's inner than to his outer religious life.

"Our Father, which art in heaven." These words say to us, "Go within!" They remind us that our home is with our Father.

God lives in Infinity. Infinity, then, is where we should seek Him. Jesus is hinting here that we should pray to God for much more than His help with mundane problems. God has far more to give us than the fulfillment of our earthly desires. By addressing Him as our "Father," we are reminded that we are His children, and have an eternal right, as well as a duty, to know Him.

"Hallowed be Thy name." God's name is hallowed enough already, surely, without the addition of good wishes from His human children! What is asked of us here is that we ourselves think of Him always with devotion, and speak His name with reverence. We are asked to recognize Him as the supreme good in our lives. It is we, in our thoughts of Him, who must hold His name hallowed.

"Name" has also, however, a deep mystical significance. It means God's "Word": the *Amen*, or *Aum*. God's eternal "name" is the great sound out of which all creation appeared. This Cosmic Sound is also known as the Holy Ghost. To speak God's name with deep devotion means to merge oneself in that infinite sound.

"Thy kingdom come." God's "kingdom" is the heaven of cosmic consciousness. These words are therefore a prayer for spiritual enlightenment. They are not a prayer that God establish some sort of

paradise on earth. "Thy kingdom come" expresses a longing for the true paradise of divine bliss.

"Thy will be done in earth, as it is in heaven." In this verse lies the essence of all spiritual teaching. It is a view downward from above. What we commonly find instead, even in religion, is a view upwards from below.

Most people when contemplating their spiritual potential use human nature as their frame of reference. "To err is human," is a true saying, no doubt, inasmuch as many human beings do err. Most people, however, take the opposite, "To be human is to err," as true also. This is a fallacy. For mankind can rise above error and banish all delusion.

In identifying his nature with error, man commits his greatest error. Heaven, not earth, is his home. We must learn to live in the thought that in God lies our own deepest reality.

In God there is harmony. Everything in heaven moves in perfect attunement to God's will. The same might be the case here on earth, if only human beings would guide their lives by high principles, instead of identifying themselves with their egos.

Ego-centeredness commits a person to the thought of his separateness from others, and above all from God. This illusion of separateness is responsible for the greatest disharmony. The ego-centered individual might be compared to a musician who was determined to ignore the orchestra in which he was playing.

"Thy will be done in earth, as it is in heaven" refers particularly to an inner reality. It may be noted that Jesus said *"in* earth," not *"on* earth." His meaning was that we should take this teaching within, by constantly offering ourselves up — body, mind, and soul — as channels for God's grace.

"Give us this day our daily bread." Bread, here, refers to much more than food. This verse is a prayer for sustenance on every level: physical, mental, spiritual. As we need energy for our bodies, so also do we need it for our minds. Above all, we need it to reinvigorate our spiritual life. Only people of high energy can find God.

"And forgive us our debts, as we forgive our debtors." Jesus himself explains this part of the Lord's prayer. It is to the extent that we forgive others that our own sins will be forgiven.

To forgive others doesn't necessarily mean bringing oneself to approve of their actions. Nor does it mean blessing them despite their offenses, while continuing to regret the disgraceful way they treated us. It means more, too, than merely forgetting their offenses. (With passing time, people usually manage this degree of forgiveness anyway.)

To forgive means to offer up into the love of God all the hurts we receive from others. When we do so sincerely, our hearts cannot but go out to them in compassion. For at that point we see that it is they, not we, who suffer owing to their ignorance. Reflect how Jesus said on the cross, "Father, forgive them, for they know not what they do."

There is a subtle reason for saying that those who forgive will be forgiven. For to forgive others demands also that we forgive ourselves. Through sin, we have offended against our own true nature as God's children. Forgiveness means relinquishing our identity with that lower reality, and identifying ourselves with the higher one.

The famous saying, "To understand all is to forgive all," should be reversed: "To forgive all is to understand everything."

"Lead us not into temptation, but deliver us from evil." This is the most difficult part of the Lord's Prayer to understand. Can it really mean that temptation comes from God? Tests, as we know, come from God, but surely it is Satan who tempts us.

The Lord, however, sometimes places us in positions where we might find ourselves being tempted! For it is well established in spiritual tradition that man's love for God must be tried. Sometimes, the Scriptures describe these tests as coming directly from God. At other times, they describe God as giving Satan freedom, for a time, to test the devotee.

These words in the Lord's Prayer give us an opportunity to make a daily choice between Satan and God. They are a way of helping us to say, "It is You I want, Lord, not Your cosmic delusion."

"God's is the kingdom, and the power, and the glory, for ever." In the unceasing, joyful contemplation of this truth the devotee is armed to fight his way steadily through the hosts of darkness. Thereby he wins through eventually to eternal freedom in God's light and love.

Thus, through the Holy Bible, God has spoken to mankind.

Bhagavad Gita

Prayer Is Self-Offering

This passage is from the fourth Chapter, the 31st Stanza. After speaking of the importance of sacrifice (self-offering) in the spiritual life, Sri Krishna says:

"Those who partake of the nectar remaining after a sacrifice attain to the Infinite Spirit (Brahma). That person, however, who makes no sacrifices never truly succeeds in enjoying even the blessings of this material world; how, then, would it be possible for him to attain happiness in subtler realms?"

Commentary

Krishna's promise of blessings here is to those devotees who offer up to God all that they are and

111

own. Such sincere yogis are able to engage in the normal activities of life while remaining ever conscious of their inner freedom in God. Their actions are not directed by ego-consciousness, but by the awareness that everything comes from God and belongs to Him. Immersed in His blissful presence, they attain final release from delusion.

Krishna refers also here to people who act from ego-consciousness. Such people consider their talents and possessions as their own. They never think of offering anything to God. Why should they? they would demand. Isn't He prosperous enough already?

Worldly-minded people, however, never really get to enjoy even the pleasures of this world, what to speak of attaining heavenly bliss in the after-world. It is a simple fact of life, and one easily tested, that selfishness never brings lasting happiness. The irony is that people justify their selfishness by claiming their "right" to personal happiness! The more urgently they grasp at happiness, the further and more quickly it leaps, like quicksilver, from their hands.

A generous, expansive spirit is the primary condition for true happiness. People who transcend their natural selfishness by giving of themselves to others find that they are always happy.

The true devotee, having once understood that God is everything, and that he himself is nothing, offers all to God, no longer asking anything for himself. This is not to say that he starves himself, or refrains from engaging in worthwhile activity. Rather, it means all that he does is done in conscious partnership with God. Even the pleasures of this world, such as eating wholesome food, relaxing in good company, and enjoying the beauties of Nature, are seen by him as blessings from God.

To eat food without first offering it to God is, so the Indian Scriptures say, to eat sin. To enjoy anything without sharing one's enjoyment with the divine consciousness within is to commit a sin. For sin is that thought or deed which holds man apart from God.

And yet, the good things of earth can all be enjoyed without sin, and may actually help one on the path to God. All one need do is enjoy them as blessings shared with Him, because derived from Him.

Thus, Krishna in the Bhagavad Gita, with supreme mastery of the intricacies of the spiritual life, resolves one of the deepest problems on the path: how to harmonize human with divine nature.

For centuries, self-abnegation has been the accepted criterion of spirituality. Self-denial, however, may easily result in the thought that God is an intolerant Lord, judgmental and filled with wrath. How sweet, by contrast, is the Bhagavad Gita's explanation of the way of transformation: not by suppressing human nature, but by calling to the divine light to shine into every corner of our lives! God is never wrathful. His nature is Love.

To know Him, then, we must love Him above all. We must give to Him of ourselves. Those who ask only that He, or that life, shower *them* with blessings instead never get to enjoy the fruits of prayer in this life, and fail also to attain them in a heavenly state of existence after death.

Thus, through the Bhagavad Gita, God has spoken to mankind.

The Power of Prayer

Bible

The Power of Faith

These passages are taken from the Gospel of St. Matthew, Chapter 7, Verse 7; and from Chapter 21, Verses 21 and 22:

> "Ask, and it shall be given you; seek, and ye shall find; knock, and it shall be opened unto you....
>
> "Verily I say unto you, If ye have faith, and doubt not ... if ye shall say unto this mountain, Be thou removed, and be thou cast into the sea; it shall be done.
>
> "And all things, whatsoever ye shall ask in prayer, believing, ye shall receive."

Commentary

Jesus is saying here that to pray effectively one must believe deeply in the power of prayer. He uses two words that people often, but mistakenly, use interchangeably: belief, and faith. These words, though similar in meaning, indicate a progression.

First in the progression comes belief. Belief implies hypothetical acceptance, but not certainty. Faith, on the other hand, is that certainty which comes after one's belief has been tested.

I may entrust precious jewels to someone, for example, telling myself, "I believe in him." At what point, then, can I truthfully say, "I have faith in him"? Only after his honesty has been proved. Religious belief, similarly, may inspire us to seek direct spiritual experience, but faith comes later. It can only come after some measure of experience has been attained.

Is it really possible, one may wonder, by faith alone to perform miracles? We must understand that what faith does is simply attune us to a greater power. Few people realize that they never accomplish anything in their lives by their own power alone. We partake of an infinite reality. Every deed, every thought, every feeling is connected to some aspect of that greater reality, and strengthened by it. Our actions gain power from those aspects of the larger reality, whether positive or negative, to which they are attuned.

The person who is vigorously and creatively in step with the consciousness of his age may achieve great fame and success in his lifetime. If he does so, it will not be by his power alone. It will also be due to the added energy of countless others around him.

That person, on the other hand, who seeks truth, not popularity, may remain relatively unknown during his lifetime, although recognition may come to his work even many years after his death. He, too, however, must have support and inspiration for his thoughts — if not from the people of his day, then from subtler minds, or even from subtler realms of reality.

For no man stands alone. We all draw our strength from those levels of reality to which we personally relate.

Miraculous powers result when the human will is reinforced by the almighty, divine will. One who elects to live deeply for God will find the divine consciousness ever reinforcing him. An event regarded by others as miraculous will be for him, therefore, perfectly natural.

Belief is not radically different from faith. The difference is one of degree. Without realized faith, but with firm belief, one may still perform wonders, according to one's measure of inner attunement.

There is a vast difference between a sincere desire to learn the truth of a matter, and that cynical attitude which assumes that there is no truth to be learned. True belief is sustained by sincere questioning, but undermined by prejudgment.

Belief should be as affirmative as possible. To pray effectively, we should attune our prayers to God's will for us. We should believe deeply that whatever we ask of Him, *if it is in keeping with His will*, is already ours.

The best kind of belief is that of complete, all-surrendering trust in God's love for us, without asking for any outward demonstration of His love. As Jesus put it, "Your Father knoweth what things ye have need of, before ye ask him." (Matthew 6:8)

Faith is the greatest power in the universe. Our need is to open ourselves ever more fully to its flow.

Thus, through the Holy Bible, God has spoken to mankind.

Bhagavad Gita

Prayer and Concentration

This passage is from the sixth Chapter, the 26th Stanza:

> *"Whenever the mind, fickle and restless, wanders off from its concentration, let the meditating yogi withdraw it resolutely, spurning every distraction (no matter how alluring!), and bring it back again and again under the control of the Self."*

Commentary

One-pointed concentration is the essence of effective prayer. Even if we define prayer, as most people prefer to do, in more loving terms, love itself is wholehearted only when its attention is focused completely on the object of its love.

Imagine a young man telephoning his beloved and saying, "Darling, every minute that we spend apart is, for me, like an hourglass filled with soggy sand. The slowly dropping seconds seem like tired workmen, reluctantly turning spadefuls of dirt into a wheelbarrow. Dearest, like a parched valley yearning for revivifying rain, so my heart thirsts for that joyful moment when next we meet!... Meet: *meat!* — Oh, my God, the lamb chops! Mother made me promise to get them at the supermarket, and I forgot. What on earth can I tell her? We've guests coming to dinner in an hour. She'll absolutely *cream* me! I shouldn't be surprised if she served *me* up for the main course instead!...

"Oh, oh! I'm sorry, sweetheart; forgive me: What was I saying?"

How impressed would his sweetheart be with the poetry of his first sentences, after enduring the rest of this monologue? She might easily conclude that he'd stumbled upon them in the pages of a book, or perhaps been rehearsing them for years with other lady loves. The impact of those opening lines would be diluted, certainly, by the digression that followed them.

Are prayer and meditation so very different from this young man's case in their need for focused attention? Concentration is essential for success in any worldly undertaking. Can it be less important in man's efforts to contact the subtlest reality there is? It is not possible to win God's love, so long as one's love for Him is vague or sporadic.

The devotee must exercise constant patience and

determination. He must bring his mind back again and again to its spiritual focus. Until he learns concentration, although years pass he will find himself making no substantial progress at all.

For one's concentration to be deep and prayerful, it must spring from a consciousness of deep attunement with God. The human will, finding itself absorbed in God's will, finds itself reinforced by His infinite power. No miracle is too great for anyone whose consciousness is perfectly attuned to the divine consciousness.

To emphasize the importance of uttering one's prayers in a state of attunement, every religion traditionally ends its prayers with a one-word affirmation of inward communion. Among Hindus, this word is *Aum*. Among Jews and Christians, it is *Amen*. Among Muslims, it is *Amin*.

Amen is commonly understood to mean simply, "So be it." Its real meaning is much deeper. For *Amen*, like *Aum*, is also a word for the Holy Spirit. As we read in the Book of Revelation, "These things saith the *Amen*, the faithful and true witness, the beginning of the creation of God." (Revelation 3:14) The *Amen* is "the beginning of the creation of God" because all things were manifested out of it. It is the Cosmic Creative Vibration. Were that vibration to cease, all things would merge back into God.

The *Amen* is also spoken of as the "Word" of God. As the Bible says, in John 1:1, "In the beginning was the Word, and the Word was with God, and the Word was God." It is called the "Word" because its vibratory sound pervades the entire universe.

121

The "Amen," again, is "the faithful and true witness" because, as the sound of a motor indicates that someone is running the motor, so this Cosmic Sound testifies to the reality of God behind creation.

Aum, Amen, or *Amin* are uttered at the end of prayers to affirm that they have been spoken in the deep inner consciousness of God's Word, or Holy Ghost.

This Sacred Sound, little known to most religionists, is an eternal verity. No one can hear it if his religious practices are outward or superficial. There are techniques of yoga, however, that enable the devotee to hear, as well as to commune with, this sound. To pray effectively, one should do so while he is immersed in a state of inner communion with the Holy Ghost. To pray effectively, then, he should meditate first with deep concentration, until he feels some contact with the divine Presence. Once he absorbs himself in that inner sound, the power of his prayer will be much greater.

Prayer, Paramhansa Yogananda said, should be offered as a "loving demand." That is, one should ask with conviction, not supplicate like a beggar. "Loving demands," spoken in the vibrant consciousness of the Divine Sound within, will not only be heard by God, but will be energized and filled with His infinite power.

To achieve a divine contact, one must first discipline his mind to correct its habitual restlessness. He must bring it back repeatedly from all outward distractions. Gradually, even the most restless mind can learn to obey the guidance of the higher Self within.

Thus, through the Bhagavad Gita, God has spoken to mankind.

Part VIII

The Circle of Return

How To
Overcome Suffering

Bible

The Parable of the Prodigal Son

This passage is from the Gospel of St. Luke, Chapter 15, Verses 11-24:

"A certain man had two sons. And the younger of them said to his father, 'Father, give me the share of the property that falls to me.' And he divided his means between them.

"And not many days later, the younger son gathered up all his wealth, and took his journey into a far country; and there he squandered his fortune in loose living. And after he had spent all, there came a grievous famine over that country, and he began himself to suffer want. And he went and joined one of the citizens of that country, who sent him to his farm to feed swine. And he longed to fill himself with the pods that the swine were eating, but no one offered to give them to him.

127

"But when he came to himself, he said, 'How many hired men in my father's house have bread in abundance, while I am perishing here with hunger! I will get up and go to my father, and will say to him, "Father, I have sinned against heaven and before thee. I am no longer worthy to be called thy son; make me as one of thy hired men."' And he arose and went to his father.

"But while he was yet a long way off, his father saw him and was moved with compassion, and ran and fell upon his neck and kissed him. And the son said to him, 'Father, I have sinned against heaven and before thee. I am no longer worthy to be called thy son.' But the father said to his servants, 'Fetch quickly the best robe and put it on him, and give him a ring for his finger and sandals for his feet; and bring out the fattened calf and kill it, and let us eat and make merry; because this my son was dead, and has come to life again; he was lost, and is found.' And they began to make merry."

Commentary

In this parable, one of his most famous and beautiful, Jesus describes the soul in its eternal relationship to God.

People often pose the challenge: "If God truly loves us, how can He permit us to suffer?" People's natural tendency, because no one wants to suffer, is to seek the cause of their suffering outside themselves. One often hears the cry, "I didn't ask for this!" If they can find no one else to blame, people sometimes rage in anger against God Himself.

The truth is, however, that on certain levels of our consciousness we actually do ask for the pain we experience in our lives. In some part of ourselves, we *want* to pay for our mistakes, and to be healed of our ignorance. On a soul level, besides, we understand that no earthly suffering could approach the eons-old agony of exile from our true home in God.

Human beings experience suffering because, although created as God's children and welcome to dwell with Him forever, they have chosen to wander afar. They might have chosen, instead, to remain with Him eternally. It was only one of the sons in the parable who became prodigal.

According to orthodox Christian dogma, heaven is not man's birthright. "We are born in sin," goes the saying, "and can be saved only by accepting Jesus Christ's redemptive death on the cross."

The parable of the Prodigal Son, however, makes a powerful statement to the contrary. According to this story, we were God's children from the first. And even if we were born in sin in this earthly body, because of the physical desire of our parents, the parable still applies. For Jesus' reference here is to the soul's *first* creation.

When, indeed, were we first created? Was it only at the moment of our physical birth? Or were we first formed in eternity? Does Jesus' statement, "Before Abraham was, I am," apply only to him? Or is it an eternal truth, applicable to all?

Jesus, in the parable of the Prodigal Son, is saying that we were created the children of God. We had the choice, originally, to remain with our heavenly

Father in His infinite mansion, or to roam off into "foreign lands" of materialism.

Our choice, at some time in the distant past, must have been to leave our infinite home, and settle for egoic limitation. Cut off from our Father's home, we experienced hunger in our souls for His perfect joy. The famine suffered by the prodigal son is the unhappiness man feels when he finds himself bereft of inner nourishment. Energy has gone out from him to enjoy the things of earth, but he has received nothing back from them in return.

Jesus is saying that we can return home to God any time *we* choose. We have only to reject the lures of this world, and to turn within, in inner communion with the Lord. Jesus' beautiful promise is that God will never judge us harshly for having left Him. Quite the contrary, He will welcome us back with joy. For He is our eternal Father. What else could He do but take us back?

The choice is ours alone. Do we long for Him? Or do we want to go on suffering in our self-imposed exile, subjected continually to the indignities of an exile's lot?

If we accept the doctrine of original sin as responsible for our physical creation, we are left with no choice but to interpret the parable of the Prodigal Son as applying to a state of existence *prior to* this physical birth. To believe otherwise is to accept two mutually exclusive doctrines.

Obviously, the parable of the Prodigal Son can apply only to our creation before the present life. At some point in the past we emerged from God. We sinned by our own fault, and were impelled here by *our own* unfulfilled desires. The sin into which all men are born is their own.

When, then, did we first have the opportunity to sin? Christian dogma rejects preexistence, whether in previous physical bodies or in eternity. To the majority of present-day Westerners, reincarnation seems a fantastic doctrine. Yet it presents a logical solution to the doctrinal paradox that is posed by this great parable.

Next week we shall discuss the implications of this solution, and shall find justification for it in the Scriptures. Meanwhile, let us not lose sight of the lesson of this parable. The story is an inspiring reminder that we are eternally God's children, and that our divine destiny is to return to our lost home in Him.

As St. Augustine put it, "Father, thou hast made us for thyself, and our hearts are restless until they find their rest in Thee." God's kingdom is our true home. The realm of matter, in which the ego wanders, is forever foreign territory to the soul.

Thus, through the Holy Bible, God has spoken to mankind.

Bhagavad Gita

Go Within!

This passage is from the sixth Chapter, the 27th Stanza:

> *"Supreme blessedness is that yogi's who has completely calmed his mind, controlled his ego-active tendencies* (rajas), *and purged himself of desire, thereby attaining oneness with Brahma, the Infinite Spirit."*

Commentary

Jesus in the parable of the Prodigal Son described as a return home the repentant soul's return to God. The Prodigal Son, in leaving home, thought to create a new home for himself in foreign lands. But he couldn't do so. The home he had left behind remained his only home. When he returned to his father, he didn't "go out" from those lands; he came back to where he belonged. The implication is obvious.

Where can we turn, to return to God? Jesus supplied the answer. In Luke 17:21, he said, "The kingdom of God is within." The soul is lured out of its divine home through the doorways of the senses. Attracted by the false glamour of material pleasures, it squanders its wealth of inner peace on "riotous living," as the parable puts it. Sense objects, however, and sense experiences can never give man the peace and happiness he seeks from them.

For sense objects only reflect back to him the expectations he brings to them in the first place. If he looks to them, instead of to his soul, for nourishment, he cannot but experience, sooner or later, a deep sense of inner emptiness. For in nourishing only his expectations of sense pleasures, he eventually exhausts his capacity to give to them of himself any more. Sense pleasures become stale and no longer attractive to him.

The desperation of the ego in its efforts to continue feeding its material habits, even after deriving no more satisfaction from them, is the meaning of the Prodigal Son's servitude to the farmer, and of the job the farmer gave him of feeding the swine.

The return to our home in God is a rediscovery of our spiritual center within. We need make no long voyage to reach God. We are His already! It is the focus of our attention, only, that has strayed from Him. The Bhagavad Gita makes it clear that supreme blessedness comes by redirecting our energies and attention inward: from the world of the senses to that of the Spirit.

Worldly wisdom is achieved by the acquisition of knowledge. Spiritual wisdom, on the contrary, can never be acquired. It is revealed in the soul, once the acquisitions of the ego have been shed.

Patanjali, the ancient authority on yoga, described spiritual awakening as *smriti*. *Smriti* means "memory." The mind has only to remove the obscuring fog of false self-identities: identities such as, "I am a businessman; I am rich; I am a man, a woman, an American, a Frenchman; I am old, young, victorious in life, defeated by life." These waves of outward involvement need to be stilled. Once they become calm, one's eternal reality is *remembered* at last.

"Supreme blessedness," Sri Krishna states in this passage, "comes to that yogi who has completely calmed his mind." Calmness comes with control of the feelings born of the ego-active tendency. The tendency to involve oneself in outward activities can be gradually curbed — outwardly, by directing the mind toward serviceful, ego-expanding activities; and inwardly, by offering all the fruits of one's activities to God.

Sri Krishna says that we must purge ourselves of egoic desire. Once the false notion has been shed that we *need* anything at all, we discover that we *have* perfect happiness already: that we need not seek it outside ourselves, for *we are that*!

When the soul achieves perfect rest in itself, it realizes its natural state: oneness with the Infinite Spirit. This state of supreme blessedness stands alone. There is nothing to which to compare it. It is the only Reality.

Thus, through the Bhagavad Gita, God has spoken to mankind.

Reincarnation:
Wisdom of the Ages

Bible

Reincarnation — Truth or Fallacy?

This passage is from the Book of Revelation, Chapter 3, Verse 12:

"Him that overcometh will I make a pillar in the temple of my God, and he shall go no more out."

Commentary

This is one of many verses in the Bible that refer to reincarnation. In recent years, the doctrine of reincarnation has won increasingly widespread acceptance in the West. The beauty of this passage is that it expresses the doctrine so succinctly, and in a manner so rich with meaning.

"Overcoming" is a reference to conquest over the ego, with its ceaseless demands for sense-gratification. Tests on the spiritual path are an opportunity to grow stronger in our aspiration to know God. The opportunity takes the form of a challenge: "Are you ready, on this point at least, to dismiss the power of delusion?" "Overcoming" means to free the heart from its last vestiges of desire. "Blessed are the pure in heart," as Jesus put it, "for they shall see God."

The image of a pillar suggests the straight spine and upright bearing of one whose aspirations in life are unequivocal and clear. For the devotee, as a matter of fact, it is important always to keep the spine straight, literally so. For one thing, an upright posture helps to develop will power and basic spiritual attitudes such as truthfulness and self-honesty. And in meditation, a straight spine helps one to direct his energy upward to the brain and to the Christ center.

In architecture, a pillar is used to help support something, usually a roof. In this sense, the metaphor is infelicitous. For the reference to "the temple of my God" suggests the "temple" of infinite awareness. What need has Infinity for support of any kind? The Lord is Absolute Perfection.

Pillars, however, are also held firmly in place by the buildings in which they stand. In this sense, the metaphor is valid, and fits well with the words that follow: "and they shall go no more out."

There is another, more outward justification for the image of a pillar. If we take the word "temple" in the outward sense of earthly religion, then realized masters may rightly be said to resemble pillars in the supportive role they play. For ultimately only those whose souls are united with God have the divine responsibility to uphold truth on earth, and to act as God's spokesmen to the religions of the world. Always, the true custodians of religion are the saints.

Thus, the image of a pillar aptly describes both levels of reality: in eternity, the liberated soul's unidirectional focus on God alone, and his eternal protection by God; and, here on earth, the saint's special role as a spokesman for spiritual truth.

The last part of this Scripture passage is the most interesting: the words, "and he shall go no more out." This reference to "going out" recalls naturally to mind the parable of the Prodigal Son and his going out from his father's home. The soul "goes out" from God when it first decides to explore the temptations of delusion.

Every time a person dies physically, he is given a chance to repent of his earthly follies and return to God. If he dies absorbed in the thought of God alone, then even at that hour of death he can achieve eternal freedom. If, on the other hand, he dies without having purified his heart of earthly desires, he is drawn back again to the material plane after a rest of varying duration in the astral world. Here on earth, he continues to work out his worldly desires, until liberated from them.

This second "going out" is not from the soul's home in God, but from the astral world. To "go no more out" signifies to reincarnate no more on this earth plane owing to compelling material desires. To go no *more* out, moreover, is a clear hint that the soul's return to this material level of existence is repeated again and again.

Reincarnation is one of the most ancient doctrines in religion. It is fully accepted by the adherents of Hinduism, Buddhism, and other religions. It is also hinted at in numerous places in the Bible. It was believed in and taught by some of the most revered early Church Fathers, among them Origen, the foremost theologian prior to St. Augustine.

Reincarnation has also been strongly endorsed by some of the greatest minds in Western history. The philosopher David Hume declared that this doctrine offers "the only system to which Philosophy can hearken."

Biblical passages that teach, or that strongly suggest, the doctrine of reincarnation include Job's cry, "Naked came I out of my mother's womb, and naked shall I return thither [that is to say, into another womb]." (Job 1:21)

Another passage is Matthew 17:12-13, where Jesus tells his disciples, "Elias [that is to say, the ancient prophet Elijah] is come already, and they knew him not." The Bible continues, "Then the disciples understood that he spake unto them of John the Baptist."

In Matthew 11:13-15, Jesus made the same statement even more openly: "For all the prophets and the law prophesied until John. And if ye will receive it, this is Elias [Elijah], which was for to come. He that hath ears to hear," he added, "let him hear."

Even the statement in Genesis 9:6, "Whoso sheddeth man's blood, by man shall his blood be shed," is an explanation of the divine law, and not a commandment to mankind to execute murderers. God's universal commandment, after all, is, "Thou shalt not kill." If one man kills another, he ordains similar treatment for himself, if not in this life then in another. It is the law, and not the human lust for vengeance, that must be satisfied.

In Jesus' day, reincarnation seems to have been widely accepted, judging particularly from two passages in the New Testament. In the first of these, Jesus asks the disciples, "Who do men say that I am?" And they reply, "Some say that you are Elias; others, that you must be Jeremiah, or one of the other ancient prophets." (Matthew 16:13,14)

In the second passage, the disciples, on seeing a man who had been sightless from birth, ask their Master, "Who sinned, this man, or his parents, that he was born blind?" (John 9:2)

In both cases the question of reincarnation is raised openly. In neither case, however, does Jesus repudiate the doctrine, as duty must have compelled him to do, had it been false.

The clearest and most succinct expression of this doctrine in any Scripture, surely, is the one contained in this week's passage: "Him that overcometh will I make a pillar in the temple of my God, and he shall go no more out."

The pathway of the soul is like a vast circle, curving outward from God, then turning back eventually to its completion in Him. The size of the circle, and the duration of each soul's journey, depend on the individual. Human beings are both blessed and burdened with free will. One may play with worldly desires as long as he likes, returning here even millions of times, if he so chooses. Eternally, the choice is man's.

There is not only earthly fulfillment in this

return, however. There is also great pain and suffering — not of God's choosing, but of our own. By returning to matter, we choose material limitation, and alienation from our Creator and only true Friend. Paramhansa Yogananda remarked once that this is why the first act of babies, when they are born, is to cry.

It was to awaken in his disciple the desire for perfect joy in God that Krishna said so urgently, "O Arjuna, *get away* from My ocean of suffering and misery!" The goal of life is to overcome our ego-limitations, and to soar in endless freedom in Spirit. Once this blissful state is achieved, our souls become eternally established in God.

Fulfilling the commandment, "Be ye therefore perfect, even as your Father which is in heaven is perfect" (Matthew 5:48), the liberated soul need never more "go out" into limitation. It will return here only if it chooses, out of divine love for its struggling brothers and sisters, to help them to come to Him.

Thus, through the Holy Bible, God has spoken to mankind.

Bhagavad Gita

Can You Recall Your Distant Past?

This passage is from the fourth Chapter, the fifth Stanza:

"The blessed Lord said, 'Arjuna, you and I have passed through many births. I know all of them, though you, O chastiser of foes, recall them not.'"

Commentary

Arjuna, before whose mighty sword of discrimination the forces of delusion were in full flight, had yet to achieve final spiritual victory. He had not yet realized the indwelling, divine Self.

Only in the state of perfect dispassion, of divine nonattachment to the present incarnation, or to any previous incarnation, does the soul remember all its lives on earth as well as in the astral world.

Krishna spoke of *knowing* all previous births, rather than "remembering" them. To him, time itself existed always in the present tense. In his cosmic consciousness, moreover, he knew the past lives of all beings. His awareness was far more than memory; it was omniscience.

In the above passage we see the importance of accepting the authority of enlightened souls, rather than relying on human opinions to lead us to wisdom. Most intelligent of men is he who submits his intelligence to the guidance of wisdom, as embodied in a Self-realized master. For Truth can never be created: It can only be perceived.

Arguments, even evidence, in favor of reincarnation are often dismissed airily with the words, "Oh, but it doesn't necessarily follow." There have, for example, been numerous cases of children who seem to have been able to remember in detail certain experiences from their past lives. They supplied little-known bits of information that were subsequently verified. Some of them even remembered words from languages to which, in this lifetime, they had never been exposed. As often as such accounts appear, however, skeptics have dismissed them, saying, "Oh, but it doesn't necessarily follow that those were memories." The supposed recollections might have been suggested by something the children heard. Or they might have been the result of telepathic influence. They might even be explainable by vaguer concepts such as "racial memory."

Such alternatives seem considerably more far-fetched than the simple explanation that the children did, in fact, remember their former lives. The only imaginable advantage to these alternatives is that they absolve those who offer them from having to think any more about the subject. No doubt these people imagine that by ignoring their own spiritual bewilderment it will never rise up again to haunt them.

In fact, it may as well be admitted that virtually *nothing* necessarily follows from anything else, if one is sufficiently determined not to accept it. The validity of an argument depends not only on its internal logic, but also on a person's receptivity to it. If one doesn't want to accept it, he will produce so many counter-arguments that the central issue will end up getting buried in the dust of confusion.

Logic is, at best, a vicarious approach to truth. It touches only the intellect, but not one's actual state of awareness. Every issue, virtually, can be debated from different sides with a fair degree of intelligence, leaving the truth forever untouched.

Experience, then, is the only definitive basis on which to judge reality. This is why Krishna's simple answer to Arjuna is so effective. Arjuna had questioned his teacher's claim to remember things he had done long before his present birth. Krishna offered no lengthy arguments in favor of reincarnation. He replied simply, "I know my past births, and I know also yours."

The calm certainty of great masters in their spiritual wisdom is what lifts their teachings above the labored arguments of theologians. Unlike Arjuna, "the chastiser of foes," a true master feels no need to do battle for truth. What he says is for our benefit, if we choose to listen — and if, as Jesus put it, we have "ears to hear."

Wise is the devotee who, when confronted with a new teaching, doesn't ask himself first, "What do I think of it?" but rather, "What have great masters said on the subject? What has the wisdom of the ages to say about it?"

Thus, through the Bhagavad Gita, God has spoken to mankind.

Karma and
Soul-Release

Bible

Action and Reaction: The Law of Karma

This passage is from the Epistle of St. Paul to the
Galatians, Chapter 6, Verse 7:

> *"Be not deceived; God is not mocked: for
> whatsoever a man soweth, that shall he also reap."*

Commentary

This oft-quoted passage is a beautifully explicit,
and at the same time simple, description of the law
of karma.

Karmic law states that Nature responds in kind
to every action; that the past, present, and future of
each individual, and of everything in the universe,
are parts of a single continuity, like the links in a
chain.

Karma is the natural corollary to the doctrine of

reincarnation. Together, these doctrines explain life's countless anomalies: the effortless attainment, on the part of some people, of wealth, success, and good health; and the poverty, failure, and ill health that pursue others from birth no matter how hard they struggle to hoist themselves out of the quicksands of their misfortune.

Either there is a reasonable purpose to life's tapestry, or else all is pure chance, and the threads of events roam back and forth haphazardly with neither cause nor consequence. If indeed some purpose exists, then the law of karma merely fills out more completely a picture that we all instinctively recognize and accept. Certainly, people behave as though they expected their actions to bear at least some kind of fruit.

If, however, life is meaningless, as so many modern thinkers claim, then we may as well throw all caution to the winds. For in this case, life gives us carte blanche to behave entirely as we please, and to entertain no sense of responsibility for anything.

The fact is, even the most extreme exponents of meaninglessness believe that the individual is responsible at least for his own well-being. They deny only his need to consider the well-being of others. Thus, these existentialist philosophers — not much less so than anyone else — cannot but recognize the fact that some sort of connection exists between action and its self-completing consequences.

The law of karma takes the observable consequences of action to their logical conclusion. This law is based on the demonstrable fact that no action is an isolated event. An act is inevitably influenced by many causes. It produces in its turn, not one, but an infinity of results. The law of karma displays a unity throughout the universe, where, to anyone gazing only at isolated events, chaos may appear to reign.

The law of karma embraces every level of reality. Even Newton's law of physics, "For every action, there is an equal and opposite reaction," is a karmic law.

Whatever we do in our lives bears commensurate results not only in terms of what we ourselves hope to accomplish, but in terms of moral truth.

If we go against cosmic law, then exactly to the extent and in the manner in which we have erred, we attract retribution. And if our actions support the law, then we attract compensation, in terms of greater harmony and fulfillment in our lives. If, for example, we extend help to others, then we attract help in return — if not from them, then from others.

A beautiful feature of the karmic law is its perfect justice. How often in life do we extend help to others only to be misunderstood by them, or blamed, in return! Under the karmic law, however, no good deed is ever wasted; no bad deed is ever uncorrected.

St. Paul addressed the typical attitude of people who view their individual acts as isolated events, failing to look beyond them to the broad tapestry into which their lives, like threads, are woven. Foolish people, ignoring the importance of the larger picture of reality, contribute nothing to it. They imagine that they live in a purely personal reality, and deceive themselves into thinking that what goes unnoticed by man will not be noticed by God. God, as St. Paul said, is not mocked.

We can never act apart from the Lord. Nor can we act apart from His cosmic law. Our duty to Him, to the universe, and also to ourselves, is to contribute to the overall harmony and beauty of His creation, and to the well-being of His creatures.

Only by reincarnation can the karmic law be justified. For only thus can coherent patterns of cause and effect be established. If, on the other hand, the fruits of action are reaped randomly by anyone who happens to get in the way of the flow of energy, then we are dealing not with a law, but with Chaos. Without reincarnation, it would be impossible to explain life's countless anomalies.

Why are some babies born healthy, and others, sickly? Why is virtue so often unrewarded in life, while those who "inherit the earth" are so frequently the sinful? The traditional explanation of religious people, that "God's will is unfathomable," is offered only to silence inquiry. In the same spirit, ministers used to cry from their pulpits, "If God had intended for us to fly, He'd have given us wings!" Can we seriously believe that the Lord gave us intelligence with the proviso that we not use it?

The Bible says, "Whoso sheddeth man's blood, by man shall his blood be shed." (Genesis 9:6) In the single link of the chain that is a human incarnation, we often see murderers die unpunished, and even admired and envied by all. One lifetime, however, is a very small segment in the long sequence of events in an individual's existence.

According to karmic law, every deed, both good

and bad, returns with the greatest impact to its point of origin: to those persons, in other words, who performed it in the first place. Wrong actions beget suffering. They do not always beget it immediately, however.

The threads of action and reaction continue endlessly. The tapestry is as broad and as durable as the cosmos itself. The stronger one's sense of personal "doership," the more forcefully the consequences of his deeds return back upon himself. The weaker the sense of "doership," on the other hand, the more the consequences of his deeds, too, become dispersed outward.

In the case of completely selfless actions, the good that one does accrues to all mankind. Thus, with increasing spiritual development, the thread of personal involvement becomes finer and finer until it achieves invisibility.

The ultimate goal of life is to escape the endless network of karma and reclaim our soul-freedom in God. Karmic law is a reality. While seeking guidance from it, however, in our efforts to live by right principles, we should not let our will power become paralyzed by the seemingly overwhelming influence of the law.

For God's grace is supreme. Loving dependence on Him can free one from even the direst karmic retributions. As Jesus said of the woman who had been judged a sinner, "Her sins, which are many, are forgiven; for she loved much." (Luke 7:47)

Again, there is the story in the Gospel of St. John: "And as Jesus passed by, he saw a man which was blind from his birth. And his disciples asked him, saying, Master, who did sin, this man, or his parents, that he was born blind?" (John 9:1-2) Jesus had a clear opportunity, here, to expound on the law of karma and its effects — or, alternatively, to reject this teaching outright as fallacious. Instead, he chose to concentrate on the power of God's grace to nullify karma. He replied, "Neither hath this man sinned, nor his parents: but that the works of God should be made manifest in him."

Paramhansa Yogananda once remarked, "How many people excuse themselves with the cry, 'Karma! It's my karma!' If you really love God," he continued, "dwell in the consciousness of eternal freedom in Him!"

The Bible lays great emphasis on the importance of the law. Jesus came, however, to show also that the law is only a means of purifying our hearts, in order that we might learn to love.

Love, again, is a stepping-stone to receiving grace. And grace brings to the soul the highest reality of all: perfect union with God.

Thus, through the Holy Bible, God has spoken to mankind.

Bhagavad Gita

The Path to Freedom

This passage is from the fourth Chapter, the eighteenth Stanza:

> *"He who beholds inaction in action, and action in inaction, is wise among men; he is one with the Spirit; he has attained the true goal of action (perfect freedom)."*

Commentary

This most important teaching on the law of karma concerns the problem of how to get off the wheel of rebirth (as Buddha described it), and achieve freedom in the Infinite.

Karma means, quite simply, *action.* If action binds us to the wheel of rebirth, one might ask if the way to get off that wheel is not to stop acting.

Freedom, however, as the Bhagavad Gita explains in many passages, lies not in refraining from action, but in acting with a sense of *inner* freedom.

In any event, it would be impossible to refrain from acting while remaining centered in ego-consciousness. For in this case even inaction is only another kind of action. One's thoughts and feelings continue. Suppression builds up inner pressure, to the point where at last it may cause an explosion.

Even the thought, "I am *not* acting," is a kind of action. Energy, whether kinetic or potential, is always energy.

Then what about the state of coma? Even in this case, the ego clings tenaciously to the body. Nor is suicide an escape, for physical death is survived by the ego. Its rejection of earthly existence, moreover, is also a form of action — one, moreover, that will require additional hard work to expiate.

The Bhagavad Gita repeatedly counsels man to act joyfully, without attachment. Western critics who speak of Hinduism as a passive religion greatly misunderstand this central point in the Hindu teachings.

How is it possible to act enthusiastically, yet at the same time with nonattachment? This stanza of the Gita gives us the answer. It tells us to see inaction in action, and action in inaction.

The enthusiasm called for on the spiritual path is not emotional. It is motivated by inner soul-joy. God is Bliss itself. At the same time, active as He is in the ever-changing universe, He remains forever changeless and unaffected. Although dwelling *in* everything, He yet is never *of* anything. Divine inaction lies at the heart of every action in the universe.

To see inaction in action can be understood in a personal as well as in an abstract sense. The yogi sees activity as merely manifesting itself through him; he never sees himself as the doer. And he also sees all movement in the universe as proceeding from the heart of Eternal Stillness. Movement itself, he realizes, is an illusion. Everything is but a dream in the forever unmoving consciousness of the Infinite.

To see the opposite, action in inaction, can be understood on two levels also. First, it means to recognize in outward inactivity a form of activity. Second, it means to realize that *effective* action springs from a center of stillness.

The worldly person identifies productive activity with a flurry of outward movement. Actually, however, the most creative contributions in history have always proceeded from inner calmness. Great deeds are never done by those who run about restlessly in circles.

Worldly people have difficulty accepting meditation as a constructive activity. The yogi, however, sees meditation as the highest activity of all. It frees the mind from useless attachments, and directs it away from useless pursuits. The yogi, filled with the bliss of inner communion with God, does everything in a spirit of freedom. Any karmas that he initiates accrue, then, to the welfare of others. They have no further binding effect on himself.

Thus, through the Bhagavad Gita, God has spoken to mankind.

Part IX

The Redemption

"What if I Fail Spiritually?" — The Divine Answer

Bible

The Second Coming

This passage is from the Gospel of St. Matthew, Chapter 25, Verses 1-13:

"Then shall the kingdom of heaven be likened unto ten virgins, which took their lamps, and went forth to meet the bridegroom.

"And five of them were wise, and five were foolish.

"They that were foolish took their lamps, and took no oil with them:

"But the wise took oil in their vessels with their lamps.

"While the bridegroom tarried, they all slumbered and slept.

"And at midnight there was a cry made, Behold, the bridegroom cometh; go ye out to meet him.

"Then all those virgins arose, and trimmed their lamps.

"And the foolish said unto the wise, Give us of your oil; for our lamps are gone out.

"But the wise answered, saying, Not so; lest there be not enough for us and you: but go ye rather to them that sell, and buy for yourselves.

"And while they went to buy, the bridegroom came; and they that were ready went in with him to the marriage: and the door was shut.

"Afterward came also the other virgins, saying, Lord, Lord, open to us.

"But he answered and said, Verily, I say unto you, I know you not.

"Watch, therefore, for ye know neither the day nor the hour wherein the Son of man cometh."

Commentary

Paramhansa Yogananda gave this passage a very different interpretation from that given it traditionally. He saw it not as a prophecy of Jesus' physical return to earth — an event that is expected to be witnessed by all humanity — but rather as a description of the advent of Christ Consciousness in the souls of true devotees.

The ten virgins, Yogananda said, symbolize the different types of devotees. He described them as women because, in mystical tradition, God is spoken of as the "Bridegroom," the only "positive," or male, principle in the universe. In relation to Him, all souls are "female." The attitude needed for spiritual awakening, in other words, is one of joyful surrender and receptivity to the inflow of divine grace.

The lamps, here, represent the various forms and practices of religion — not outward rituals only, but also techniques of concentration and meditation. The oil in the lamps represents devotion. The wicks represent the heart.

The foolish virgins are those deluded devotees who imagine that rituals and formal practices, whether outward or inward, will suffice in themselves to win God's favor. A lamp without oil cannot burn. Spiritual practices, too, if engaged in without the "oil" of devotion, will lack the fire necessary to win the grace of Him, Who is Love Itself.

The coming of the Bridegroom signifies the descent of God into the soul, through the Christ Consciousness. No one may know when the Bridegroom will come. God tests us to determine the depth of our love for Him. It is important therefore that we be ever attentive, lest grace descend and we be found lacking the devotion to receive it.

It seems hardly likely that Jesus intended these ten virgins to represent the whole human race. Five of them, in fact, had to go off in search of other people to give them oil. Nor, for that matter, does his image here suggest only the individual's search for enlightenment. The ten virgins suggest, rather, a group of disciples.

There are times when God's grace descends to earth as a special ray. It is brought by a great Savior, like Jesus, for the salvation of many. This divine descent, or *avatara* as it is called in Sanskrit, is a special act of dispensation by God. Those people who are at least outwardly receptive to the ray of an *avatara* may become students, or perhaps only admirers and supporters, of the descending master. Only those true devotees, however, who receive him deeply into their consciousness are his disciples. It was to his disciples that Jesus, now that his earthly mission was nearing its end, was referring in this story.

He was telling them to be watchful and inwardly ever-prepared to receive the Christ Consciousness, lest it descend upon them unexpectedly. Woe to the disciple, if his devotion is too weak to soar in response to God's call! It may be a long time ere the Lord sends such a ray to earth for him again.

Special acts of divine dispensation are not for all mankind, but for those only who are specially called. As Jesus put it in Matthew 24:40 and 41, "Then shall two be in the field; the one shall be taken, and the other left. Two women shall be grinding at the mill; the one shall be taken, and the other left." One's readiness to be called is not determined by his outward position in life, nor by any work that he does, however outwardly religious. God watches the heart.

Meditation is a process of increasing one's inner receptivity. This, as we said, is why the disciples are described here as virgins. And that also is why women, more receptive by nature, are more often attracted to the spiritual path than are men.

It all balances out, however. For once masculine energy becomes truly dedicated to a course of action, it often does so with great fervor. Women, often, are impeded by attachment to little things.

Thus, just as masculine energy needs to be balanced with feminine energy, so also the feminine energy needs to be infused by the masculine. For women to advance far on the path, they need to balance their receptive, feminine energy with forceful, more masculine vigor.

In our souls we are neither men nor women, but a harmonious whole that may be described as equally masculine and feminine. The ideal human being is lovingly open and receptive to that which flows into him from above; firm in his commitment to truth, and in his rejection of error; and a pillar of strength and wisdom for those less experienced than himself, who aspire to grow in the Spirit.

Jesus made the statement in Matthew 24:34, "Verily I say unto you, This generation shall not pass, till all these things be fulfilled." We see here again that his reference was not to an outward Second Coming. Numerous generations have passed since he spoke those words. Outwardly, his prophecy has yet to be fulfilled. Indeed, it might be said to have been discredited by the fact that it didn't take place within the time frame he assigned to it. Inwardly, however, his prophecy was indeed fulfilled, and during the lifetime of his listeners. Moreover, although after nearly two thousand years the nations of the earth have yet to behold him "in the clouds," sincere devotees of every race and nation *have* beheld the Christ in their own souls.

Jesus stated this truth even more forcefully in Matthew 16:28, where he said, "Verily I say unto you, There be some standing here, *which shall not taste of death*, till they see the Son of man coming in his kingdom." In fact, true disciples would not taste of death at all, since with his coming they attained eternal life.

Jesus described his Second Coming in these words: "For as the lightning cometh out of the east, and shineth even unto the west, so shall also the coming of the Son of man be." (Matthew 24:27) The east of the body — *Kedem* in the ancient Hebrew, meaning, "that which lies before" — is the forehead, where the devotee beholds the light of God in meditation. The divine light spreads backward ("even unto the west"), filling the brain, then downward into the entire body. As Jesus put it similarly, at the beginning of his mission: "The light of the body is the eye. If therefore thine eye be single, thy whole body shall be full of light." (Matthew 6:22)

Thus, the devotee realizes that he is, and has always been, a child of the divine light. Never again will darkness and delusion have the power to claim him.

Watch, therefore, and pray, for none of us knows when the Christ will descend upon him. When he comes it will be, as St. Paul said, "like a thief in the night" (I Thessalonians 5:2) — not with outward lightning, trumpets, and crashing chords, but silently, invisibly save only to those whose thoughts are deeply attentive, rapt in deep communion with Him.

Thus, through the Holy Bible, God has spoken to mankind.

Bhagavad Gita

Hope for the Fallen

This passage is from the sixth Chapter, the 37th to the 47th Stanzas:

Arjuna:

> *"What is the fate of him who strives with faith,*
> *But fails, and loses heart; or even falls*
> *From holiness, missing the perfect rule?*
> *Like the rent cloud that quickly vanishes,*
> *Is he not lost, abandoning the Way?*
> *Remove, O Krishna, my uncertainties!*
> *No one but Thou canst banish my grave doubts.*

Krishna:

> *"Arjuna, none who works for self-redemption*
> *Will ever meet an evil destiny!*
> *Not here on earth, nor in the other world*

Will he encounter sorrow and destruction.

"A fallen yogi, when he dies, attains
The heavenly regions of the virtuous!
Many the years he dwells there, joyfully.
And when at last he must return to earth,
His past true deeds will cause him to take birth
In some pure, noble-minded family,
Happy in virtue and prosperity.

"Even it may be that he will take birth
Into the home of yogis, calm and wise:
Enlightened souls! Ah, but this kind of birth
Is all too rarely come by here on earth!

"Returning here, his good deeds of the past
Awaken in his heart the urge to seek
His former path with ever greater zeal,
Determined more than ever, now, to reach
The one true goal of life: Eternal Bliss.

"Past yoga practice, like an unseen tide,
Propels him forcefully upon his Way.
Even that man who deeply longs to know
The subtle yoga path is more advanced
Than those who merely practice outward rites,
Or follow Scripture for their private gain.

"By diligently purging self of sin
(An end achieved at last by all who strive),
The yogi, countless rebirths ended, dwells
Forever in Supreme Beatitude!

"Greater the yogi is than they who quell
Their senses with ascetic discipline:
Greater than they who seek to plumb the depths

Of truth by reasoning and wise dispute:
Greater than they who seek by works alone
To impress the Lord, who is Himself those works!
Be thou therefore a yogi, O Arjuna!

"He who absorbs his mind and soul in Me,
Unceasingly established in My rest,
Know him to be, among all yogis, best."

Commentary

Many harbor the secret doubt: "What if I fail spiritually?"

During the Gold Rush days of 1849, there were many who left everything behind to seek their fortune. Forsaking home and even family, they came adventuring for gold in California. Many of them ended up not rich, but destitute.

Is the spiritual search as unreliable as finding gold? Devotees ask themselves, "What if I fall from the path? Will my fate be worse than if I had never tried at all? Will God punish me for my failure? Will my lot be even worse, perhaps, than that of worldly people who never tried at all?"

A certain amount of apprehension does no harm. It may even prod one to increase his spiritual efforts. Smugness is not an aid to security, but a threat. And tepidity is one of the main reasons devotees fall from the path. The Scriptures warn against the danger of lukewarm devotion, as Jesus did in the parable of the Ten Virgins.

Fear, however, is an obstacle on the spiritual path, as in every undertaking in life. It can paralyze effort, and may even act as a magnet that attracts the very results one fears. There is no cause to fear, moreover.

What really *is* the fate of one who takes up the spiritual path, but later returns to a worldly life? Is it worse to fall spiritually than never to have tried in the first place?

The stern warning of the parable of the Ten Virgins was not intended to discourage. The five foolish virgins ended up being told by the Bridegroom, "I know you not," but at least they were five, out of many, who had aspired to marry him. Their chance would come again — if not in this life, then in the next, or in other future lives. God is a God of love, not of pique at human slights!

How beautiful, then, are Krishna's words of reassurance in this great passage of the Bhagavad Gita! No right effort, he assures us, is ever lost. As he promised also elsewhere: "Even a little bit of the practice of this religion (of inner communion) will save you from dire fears and colossal sufferings." (II:40)

Thus, through the Bhagavad Gita, God has spoken to mankind.

Practicing the Presence of God

Bible

The Social Way to Redemption

This passage is from the Gospel of St. Matthew, Chapter 25, Verses 34-40:

"Then shall the King say unto them on his right hand, Come, ye blessed of my Father, inherit the kingdom prepared for you from the foundation of the world:

"For I was an hungred, and ye gave me meat: I was thirsty, and ye gave me drink: I was a stranger, and ye took me in:

"Naked, and ye clothed me: I was sick, and ye visited me: I was in prison, and ye came unto me.

"Then shall the righteous answer him, saying, Lord, when saw we thee an hungred, and fed thee? or thirsty, and gave thee drink?

"When saw we thee a stranger, and took thee in? or naked, and clothed thee?

*"Or when saw we thee sick, or in prison, and
came unto thee?*

*"And the King shall answer and say unto
them, Verily I say unto you, Inasmuch as ye have
done it unto one of the least of these my brethren,
ye have done it unto me."*

Commentary

Jesus was teaching his disciples to expand their
perception of his inner reality, and not to limit it to
his little physical body, in which they saw the divine
consciousness so beautifully manifested to human
eyes.

A perfected master is fully awake in the
consciousness of God. The Lord, however, through
the infinite Christ Consciousness, is actively present
also, if still hidden or asleep, in every atom of
creation.

God's manifestation in creation may be described
as the embers of a smoldering fire: concealed in
most places by ashes; here and there glowing dimly;
and in one or two places, burning brightly. To
paraphrase the Indian Scriptures, God sleeps in the
minerals, dreams in the plants, begins to stir in the
animals, and in man is engaged in trying to shake off
slumber. Only in the masters is God fully awake,
and fully Self-aware.

Redemption is not a matter of rescue and
transportation to a better location. As Jesus put it
with wry humor, the divine kingdom is not to be
found by going off in search of it, nor by pointing
eagerly and crying, "Lo here!" or, "Lo there!" "The

kingdom of God," he stated, "is within." (Luke 17:21)

More exactly, the kingdom of God is found *by going within*. For in demolishing the ramparts of egoism, one finds his consciousness expanding out into an identity vaster than he could have ever imagined. Redemption means escape from the confining walls of egoism, and discovering an infinite reality in God.

There are two ways to achieve this expansion of consciousness. One is, in deep meditation, to rise above ego-consciousness. The other is to serve God in others. These two paths are not mutually exclusive. Rather, they complement each other, each balancing and reinforcing the other.

It is the social way to cosmic consciousness that Jesus is describing in this passage. His words are a stirring answer to anyone who imagines that, to achieve salvation, all that is necessary is to believe in Christ. Those in the story who were deemed worthy of salvation didn't even realize that it was Christ they were serving in the hungry, the thirsty, and the rest. The important thing, Jesus said, was the fact that they had served. By their active expression of compassion, their hearts' sympathies expanded as a matter of course. Inwardly identified with others' well-being, they gradually came to feel a deep identity with all.

In whatever way we expand our self-identity, the way of redemption lies in the expansion itself. It matters not whether we understand the theological implications involved. The redeemed souls in the story were not even aware that it was Christ they had been serving. Yet they found Him, not through creeds, but through love.

Thus, through the Holy Bible, God has spoken to mankind.

Bhagavad Gita

See God in Everything

This passage is from the sixth Chapter, the 30th to the 32nd Stanzas:

> *"One who beholds My presence everywhere,*
> *And all things dwelling equally in Me,*
> *He never loses loving sight of Me,*
> *Nor I of him, through all eternity.*
>
> *"That yogi finds security in Me,*
> *Who, though his days be rushed and action-filled,*
> *Is anchored inwardly, at rest in Me,*
> *And worships Me in every living form.*
>
> *"That one, Arjuna, is the best of men,*
> *And truest he, of yogis, whose heart feels*
> *The joys of all, their pains, their searing griefs,*
> *With equal care as though they were his own."*

Commentary

How beautifully reminiscent this passage is of the teachings of Jesus! We saw this teaching in the words, "Inasmuch as ye have done it unto one of the least of these my brethren, ye have done it unto me." We find it also in that passage where a certain lawyer asked Jesus, "Master, which is the great commandment in the law?" And Jesus answered him, "Thou shalt love the Lord thy God with all thy heart, and with all thy soul, and with all thy mind. This is the first and great commandment. And the second is like unto it, Thou shalt love thy neighbour as thyself. On these two commandments hang all the law and the prophets." (Matthew 22:36-40)

A precept common to all religions is the advice, "Do unto others as you would have them do unto you." This might be taken cynically, as advice on how to get the best out of others! What is really meant, however, is that we should see ourselves in all, for the deep reason that, in Spirit, we are already one with them.

Krishna, in speaking of the yogi who sees God in everything, and everything in God, was referring to one who has actually attained God-realization. Yet his teaching is important also for people on all levels of spiritual attainment.

How many people bemoan God's absence from their lives — His seeming indifference to them during their misfortunes — His apparently determined silence when they pray to Him! Sri Krishna here reveals the secret for winning a divine response: *Practice* God's presence! Call to Him not merely during hours of urgent need, when you've exhausted your own resources. Share your every thought with Him, your lightest whims, your joys, your disappointments.

People normally think, "*I* am acting; *I* am enjoying"; or, when things go badly, "*I* am disappointed." The devotee should think rather, "Lord, *we* are acting together. Every joy, every disappointment that I feel is ours, not mine alone."

Again, people normally think of God in the third person. Thus, if they want to include Him in their actions, they will think, "*He* is acting with me." The devotee must school himself rather to think "*You*," not, "*He*." He must talk to God as his dearest Friend. He may even scold God sometimes, as he might, with love, his own nearest and dearest.

He must strive to see in everything and in everyone the Lord's hidden presence; see all things in relation to infinity; think of God as playing "hide-and-seek" with him, so to speak, within every tree, every stone, every human being. He should view every tree, stone, and human being as part of that Infinite Reality out of which all things have come, and in which the entire universe resides.

It is with this consciousness that one should love his neighbor — not for his merely human qualities, but for the divine reality residing within him. One should love his neighbor for the fact that, in the greatness of God, he and his neighbor are one.

By practicing God's presence in this way, one soon finds that Conscious Presence with him everywhere he goes, guiding him, protecting him, and filling him with bliss ineffable.

Thus, through the Bhagavad Gita, God has spoken to mankind.

How To Find,
and Follow,
the Inner Star

Bible

What Was the Star of Bethlehem?

This passage is from the Gospel of St. Matthew, Chapter 2, Verses 1 and 2, and Verses 9-11:

> "Now when Jesus was born in Bethlehem of Judaea in the days of Herod the king, behold, there came wise men from the east to Jerusalem,
>
> "Saying, Where is he that is born King of the Jews? for we have seen his star in the east, and are come to worship him....
>
> "And, lo, the star, which they saw in the east, went before them, till it came and stood over where the young child was.
>
> "When they saw the star, they rejoiced with exceeding great joy.

"And when they were come into the house, they saw the young child with Mary his mother, and fell down, and worshipped him: and when they had opened their treasures, they presented unto him gifts; gold, and frankincense, and myrrh."

Commentary

Because the number of gifts the wise men offered was three, tradition has it that the wise men also numbered three. They had "seen his star in the east." For nearly two thousand years men have puzzled over this account. Were those wise men astrologers, and were they referring to a planet they'd seen in their charts? Evidently not, for the Bible says the star later "went before them, till it came and stood over where the young child was."

Was the star, then, a comet, as many have conjectured — perhaps an earlier appearance of Halley's comet? But then, why did the wise men refer to it as *"his"* star? More puzzling still, why does the account read, "It came and stood over where the young child was"? A heavenly body may appear to "stand over" a house from the vantage point of someone looking at it over the roof, but no one would mistake this appearance for reality. He'd know without testing that, a few feet away, the same heavenly body would seem to be shining over some other object.

Is this story, then, only a beautiful fable? It might indeed seem so — were it not for one particular spiritual truth, known only to mystics and yogis.

Jesus, in Matthew 6:22, said, "The light of the body is the eye: if therefore thine eye be single, thy whole body shall be full of light." Thus the passage reads in the Authorized, or King James, version of the Bible, and also in the original Greek. Modern translators from the Greek have, for the most part, changed that word, "single" (which gives the true meaning of the Greek, *Haplous*), to read, "If your eye is sound." Some, believers in the adage, "In for a penny, in for a pound," go even farther. They make "eye" plural. Thus, their translations read, "If your eyes are sound." They overlook a deep spiritual truth, however, in their effort to adjust the passage to what seems to them a more reasonable interpretation of its meaning.

In Revelation 22:4-5, we read, "And they shall see his face; and his name shall be in their foreheads. And there shall be no night there; and they need no candle, neither light of the sun; for the Lord God giveth them light: and they shall reign for ever and ever." God's name is written not only in, but *as* light. Letters are not needed to spell that holy name; the divine light itself *is* His signature.

The vision of the inner light comes in deep meditation. It is beheld in the center of the forehead, between the eyebrows. This is why saints in ecstasy are so often depicted gazing upward.

The wise men in the Biblical story are described as seeing the star in the East. They saw it there not only when they *were* in the East, but also after they had arrived in Palestine. "The star, which they saw in the East," says the Bible, "went before them." Yet they were traveling westward!

The Hebrew word for east, as we saw last week, is *Kedem*, "that which lies before." In several places in the Bible, this word is used in reference to the forehead. The "star in the east," then, was a star that the wise men saw in their foreheads.

The divine light is the reality behind the atoms of matter, the subtle vibration of which matter is but a manifestation. Matter, as modern physics teaches also, is energy. An enlightened saint lives consciously in that light. He has no need for the light of this world. To his gaze, the darkness of earth is ever illumined by God's light.

The vision of light in the forehead takes shape, once the mind is deeply concentrated. It becomes what mystical tradition calls "the single eye," "the third eye," or, in yoga teachings, "the spiritual eye." The two eyes of the body behold the world with dual vision, and, therefore, in relativity. The eye of the soul, however, beholds all things as belonging to the sole Reality, God.

The spiritual eye, when beheld clearly, is circular in shape, even as the eyes of the body are behind their eyelids. The spiritual eye is seen as a ring of golden light surrounding a field of intense, deep blue. *In the center of that light shines a brilliant, silvery white star.*

When the deeply meditating devotee is able to enter the golden light, he pierces the veil of space that separates the material universe from the astral universe. He beholds heaven and its angels. With even deeper meditation, he is able actually to enter those heavenly realms.

Meditating still more deeply, he enters the blue

field. Here, he experiences an even subtler level of divine manifestation — the causal world, as it is known, where the thoughts were formed out of which heaven and earth were projected. (From that level of consciousness Jesus was able to say, in Mark 13:31, "Heaven and earth shall pass away, but my words shall not pass away.")

The star at the center of the spiritual eye represents the Kingdom of God. By passing consciously through the star, the devotee soars beyond creation into infinite bliss. This, finally, is cosmic consciousness.

The description, then, that the wise men gave of a star which "stood over where the young child was," and the fact that they called it *his* star, had the deepest metaphysical meaning. They were telling "those who had ears to hear" that the birth of Jesus was an *avatara*: a descent to earth from the highest spiritual realm. Jesus, in other words, was an incarnation of God.

Many visions are vouchsafed the devotee, according to his special needs or beliefs. A Hindu may behold Krishna; a Christian, Jesus. It is interesting to note, at the same time, that not a few Hindu saints have beheld Jesus also, and have received deep inspiration from him through the experience. Of secondary interest is the fact that he has not told any of them to convert to Christianity.

God can appear in an infinity of forms, to suit the devotee's nature and needs — even as He has manifested an infinity of forms with His creation. The spiritual eye, however, does not belong to this category of vision. It is universal — as universal as the fact that people are born with physical eyes. This inner vision comes not by believing in it, nor by visualizing it. Countless devotees with no prior knowledge of it have been amazed to behold it suddenly, shining in the darkness of their closed eyes. At first they behold a dim, circular light, violet in color; then, gradually, a shining halo forms around it; later, a white dot appears in the center. When beheld perfectly, the white dot takes the form of a brilliant, five-pointed star.

With deep meditation, the devotee learns to see through the spiritual eye, even as we do through our physical eyes. In this case, what he beholds are the divine realms.

Thus, through the Holy Bible, God has spoken to mankind.

Bhagavad Gita

To Become Truly Great, Meditate on True Greatness

This passage is from the fourth Chapter, the ninth Stanza, in the poetic translation of Sir Edwin Arnold:

"Who knows the truth touching my births on earth
And my divine work, when he quits the flesh
Puts on its load no more, falls no more down
To earthly birth: to Me he comes, dear Prince!"

Commentary

When a person looks through the right end of a telescope, he sees distant things as though they were very near. Everything seems greatly magnified. If he looks through the wrong end, however, he sees even nearby objects as though from a distance, and everything greatly diminished in size.

For the person whose mind is focused inwardly on divine truths, the most exalted spiritual realms seem nearby. Even mundane realities seem to him magnified, in a sense, for he sees them as essentially divine.

For the person, however, whose mind is focused on mundane realities, spiritual realities seem impossibly alien. Material realities themselves appear somehow diminished, because perfectly ordinary and commonplace. The more a person becomes enmeshed in materialism, the less of beauty, inspiration, or meaning he sees in anything. The noblest men and women seem to him somehow unworthy of his respect. (Is he not just as good as they?) The loftiest teachings appear to him merely trite and uninteresting.

The crafty egotist's view of humanity is of a "sucker" being born every minute. And the spiritual man sees potential saints everywhere. Everyone beholds in others examples of what he himself is looking for in life.

What a person looks for in life helps also to determine what he eventually becomes. The crafty egotist, seeing all men as potential "suckers," stands not only revealed as an exploiter by nature. In the end — such is the karmic law — he will find himself exploited also. And the man who sees potential saintliness in others not only reveals his own sincere spirituality: In time, he himself will become a saint. The higher one's vision, the higher his eventual attainments.

To concentrate only on people's potential for divine achievement, however, can be discouraging if one doesn't concentrate especially on those in whom that potential has been realized: the great saints and masters. The austerity of many Christian sects in their denial of special merit to the saints would be better directed against the spiritual compromise of so many half-hearted Christians. Meditation on the saints is a way of drawing saintly qualities to oneself.

Even to contemplate the outward life of a great master is to become ennobled. To meditate on his inner spirit, then, helps one to rise much higher. One becomes united to him in Spirit, and, through him, comes closer to God.

It behooves everyone especially to contemplate the mystery of the divine incarnations on earth: the great *avataras*, such as Krishna, Buddha, and Jesus Christ. Even as the wise men came to see Jesus, having intuitively perceived in him a divinity that was not visible to ordinary men, so ought we to approach the great masters: with faith, with holy reverence, and in a spirit of utter self-offering. "Your duty as devotees," said the great master Sri Ramakrishna, "is to fall down and worship where others only bow."

It is not enough, moreover, to take the words of a great master and repeat them parrot-wise. Every sentence uttered by such a one is, potentially, a window onto infinity. It is difficult, moreover, for even masters to speak without creating at least a potential for misunderstanding. For this reason, too, their words must be contemplated deeply. Both to penetrate the veil of false understanding, and to open windows onto ever greater vistas of truth, one should meditate on the inner meaning of everything a great master says and does.

It is fruitful, for example, to take the above teaching of Krishna and apply it not only in a particular, but in an absolute sense. For it concerns not only his own births and actions in this world, but also the endless manifestations and creative expressions of the Infinite Spirit in creation. Krishna throughout the Bhagavad Gita refers to himself not only as a man and a spiritual teacher, Arjuna's guru, but also as the Infinite Spirit with which he was inwardly identified.

Thus, at whatever level we choose to touch the life and consciousness of a great master, through our attunement with him we become freed forever from our earthly limitations, and attain eternal oneness with God.

Thus, through the Bhagavad Gita, God has spoken to mankind.

The Way of the Christ: How To Find It, and How To Walk It

Bible

The Way of the True Christian

This passage is from the Gospel of St. John, Chapter 14, Verse 6:

"I am the way, the truth, and the life: no man cometh unto the Father, but by me."

Commentary

A truth is often understood more deeply if one can step back from it a little and view it from the broadest perspective. Let us, then, withdraw mentally from this oft-quoted passage, and view it in the broader context of Jesus' life and mission on earth.

How universally lovable is the image of Jesus as a baby, laid in a humble manger, adored by shepherds, angels, animals, and wise men! In that little form they beheld manifested the Divinity itself.

Artists for nearly two thousand years have devoted countless paintings to the portrayal of the Holy Family during those first days: Mary and Joseph, their eyes radiant with love and joy, gazing downward at the tiny infant. And Jesus smiling up at them with divine love and faith.

Contemplating the birth of Jesus, one feels both deep awe and deep gratitude at the thought of God's compassion in descending to earth in human form for man's salvation.

One also feels something else. Is it tenderness? solicitude? It is as though the Christ child were not only divine, but somehow human and fragile as well: a tiny baby needing its parents' loving care and protection.

A divine truth in this protective feeling makes images of the baby Jesus particularly affecting. For his birth is deeply symbolic of the birth of divine awareness within each one of us. The first stirrings of that awareness must indeed be treated with loving care and protection, as though it had the fragility of an infant. Jesus told his disciples to be ever watchful, to protect their inner awareness of God's presence lest they lose touch with it.

There is a second image that has captured the West's imagination through the ages. It is the drama of the Crucifixion. This image, too, is universally affecting. What we feel in Jesus' supreme sacrifice on the cross is very different from the tender sentiments awakened in us by contemplating his birth. We feel deep awe and gratitude still, but no longer, now, the impulse to protect. Rather, what we feel is the deep longing to *be* protected.

The Crucifixion makes us aware of the crosses each of us has to bear in his life, and of the need to depend totally on the saving power of grace.

This awareness, too, is based on a deep inner truth. For as our devotion grows, it no longer requires the same care and protection as it did at first, but becomes instead our teacher and guide. Its mission, rather, is to train us in the ways of absolute self-sacrifice, of unconditional love, and of perfect surrender to God.

Jesus' death on the cross offered to mankind, among other blessings, a symbol of the death of our own selfhood, of everything in us that is petty and self-seeking. The Crucifixion is a symbol of soul-freedom, attained through the death of attachment to everything of this world.

The feelings awakened by images of Jesus in the manger would remain on a level of mere sentiment, were they not directed toward devotion's true end: perfect surrender to God. And the feelings awakened by images of Jesus on the cross might only inspire fanaticism, were they not directed *from* the tenderness of devotion. Thus, spiritually speaking, the two images are interdependent.

In a like manner, the whole of Jesus' life may be contemplated not only from a standpoint of his individual teachings, but as a complete teaching in itself.

For the events in his life were more than occurrences in the life of an individual. From his birth to the Crucifixion, the teaching and example Jesus gave were rooted in principle, not in personality. He came to show and to exemplify "the Way, the Truth, and the Life." He *was* the divine life, personified.

Christians have mistaken his personification of the Truth for the broader, more impersonal Truth he represented. Jesus did in fact offer people the only visible alternative most of them had to the materialism of their age. It is perfectly true, moreover, that in his spirit he *was* the truth that he represented. He not only taught it: He was inwardly identified with it. For he was one with God.

The mistake people commonly make is to think of his special expression of Truth as being itself absolute. Worse still, they think of him as pitting himself against other great souls who, like him, represented the same truth. Yet other great masters, too, had followed the way to its end of total surrender to the Lord.

How did the wise men recognize him as divinity incarnate? It takes greatness to behold greatness. It takes wisdom to recognize wisdom. And it takes an awareness of God's presence within, to be aware of its manifestations without.

The Truth which Jesus represented was indeed unique. It will remain so eternally, for it represents the universal path to union with God, through direct, inner communion with the Lord. Despite the diversity of outward religious forms, the path of inner, spiritual awakening is essentially one. Jesus was a very great representative of this Truth, but happily not the only one to have appeared down the ages.

To insist that the greatness of Jesus is unique is to ignore, or perhaps only to be unaware of, the lives of other masters who have matched point for point every test of greatness that might possibly be applied to Jesus. Far from lessening his stature, moreover, the lives of those masters give added force to his life and teachings, as John the Baptist gave also by his testimony of Jesus, and as the wise men gave at his birth. Not one of those masters ever contradicted the truths that he taught. And not one master after him has spoken of him otherwise than with the highest praise, and in total agreement with everything he taught.

Jesus gave his disciples this test of true faith: "And these signs shall follow them that believe," he said. "In my name shall they cast out devils; they shall speak with new tongues. They shall take up serpents; and if they drink any deadly thing, it shall not hurt them; they shall lay hands on the sick, and they shall recover." (Mark 16:17,18) These signs are typical of the powers that we find expressed in the lives of all the great masters of past centuries: Krishna, Buddha, Shankara, Ramanuja, Chaitanya, and on down to the great masters of our times.

Most important of all, those great souls revealed the inner *qualities* of a true master, even as Jesus did: omniscience, omnipresence of consciousness; absolute love, compassion, and forgiveness; freedom from sorrow and from all negative qualities such as egotism, attachment, jealousy, desire, and hate. Like Jesus, those masters sought nothing for themselves. Like Jesus, too, their only desire was to obey God's will, and to help others to find the divine truth.

Jesus was saying, then, to follow the way that he had shown, the way that he himself represented, and of which his outward life was so marvelous an expression. His purpose was not to bind people to that expression, but rather, by their attunement with it, to fulfill his highest teaching: "Ye shall know the truth, and the truth shall make you free." (John 8:32)

Thus, through the Holy Bible, God has spoken to mankind.

Bhagavad Gita

Truth Is One; The Paths to It Are Many

This passage is from the fourth Chapter, the eleventh Stanza:

"O son of Pritha, in whatever way people accept Me, in that same way do I appear to them. For all men, in some way, pursue the path to Me."

Commentary

This stanza, with economy and divine simplicity, throws open the window onto vast vistas of truth, showing range on range of further meanings. Such, indeed, is one of the thrills of reading the Bhagavad Gita. Many lifetimes of meditation on it surely could not plumb it to its depths.

The Gita is speaking first of people who believe

in God and love Him. It then goes on to say that all other human beings, in one way or another, follow the path to God, whether they believe in Him or not. For none can live apart from Him, however much some people try to do so.

All men, moreover, are impelled in their heart of hearts toward Him. In Him awaits a fulfillment that they cannot but find, someday. For none can escape his own nature. Sooner or later all men shall have to discover who and what they really are, in their souls.

Very few people are aware of their high destiny. All, however, recognize their own dissatisfaction with the present state of affairs. They know that things ought to be better than they are. They feel that life ought to be less of a trial for them, and wish they could find it more enjoyable. Put simply, everyone wants to avoid pain and limitation, and to find happiness.

Everyone would also like to be as aware as possible of any happiness he finds. And he would like that happiness to endure; indeed, he'd like it to last forever. He may for a time give up hope of ever finding it. He may imagine that the best he can dare wish for is to reduce his suffering. Once, however, his suffering diminishes, his thoughts will turn naturally once more to the quest for happiness.

Thus were we all made. There is no one, anywhere, for whom these statements are not true, for the simple reason that all creatures were not only made by God, but exist and have their reality in His consciousness. As Jesus said, "Not a sparrow falls without His sight." Man's essential nature, and God's, are the same. And God's nature is bliss: bliss absolute, bliss ever-conscious, bliss eternal. Divine consciousness diminishes as it filters down into human nature. In this way it resembles sunlight, which is diminished in strength as it enters the earth's atmosphere. Sunlight is diminished still further as it enters the ocean, and grows increasingly dim until, at great depths, scarcely any light is visible at all.

Divine bliss, then, as it enters human consciousness, is experienced by the pure-minded as joy. As it enters natures that are more centered in their emotions, it is experienced as happiness. Those who are attached to the senses experience it as pleasure. And so on downward bliss moves, into ever denser ego-consciousness. It virtually ceases to be recognizable at the lowest levels of human awareness. Here, those people who are self-committed to spiritual darkness experience it primarily as an occasional lessening of pain.

For all creatures, the direction of their seeking is essentially the same: to escape pain and limitation on the one hand, and to find happiness on the other. They may define pain in many ways, but essentially it amounts to a lessening of whatever degree of happiness they have known in life. For intuitively they know, in their souls, that they have a right to happiness. Again, they may define limitation in countless ways, but essentially it is the constriction the soul feels in its confinement in the ego. And they may define happiness, too, in many ways, but essentially happiness is the deeper-than-conscious anticipation of the soul's return home to its lost bliss in God.

Men are coaxed forward on the path to

enlightenment by the law of karma. If they fail to act in harmony with their higher nature, they experience pain. And if they act in harmony with that nature, they experience increasing inner peace and happiness. Those who are harmonious, which is what Jesus meant by "meek" in the Beatitudes, "shall inherit the earth."

Thus, man is drawn gradually toward his true destiny, the final fulfillment of all his dreams. Willingly or unwillingly, consciously or unconsciously, on one level of existence or another, no creature can repudiate God. All tread the sure path to Him, however faltering or reluctant their footsteps. Even those people who shake their fists angrily at a God of their own fevered imaginings do so out of a frustrated desire for what they wish were the true God.

Numerous, alas, are the detours on the soul's long journey through delusion. Some people think for a time that they'll find happiness in money. Others look for it in fame, or good health, or power. They fail to understand that happiness is, in itself, intangible. It is a state of mind. As the thoughts in the brain are distinct from the brain itself, so is happiness distinct from the changing forms in which imagination clothes it.

The devotion of those who follow the path to God consciously, Krishna says, also takes many forms. He implies that devotees should accept the need of others to worship God in other ways. For people are not all alike in the inspiration they feel. Some find joy in singing to God; others, in working for Him; still others, in deeply pondering His mysteries. No one way is right for everyone.

Those who feel inspired by singing to the Lord may feel a distaste for theological discourses. And those who enjoy discussing subtle Scriptural points may feel a distaste for singing. A sweet taste can be enjoyed in many ways: as chocolate, as candy, as fresh fruits. No one way is equally pleasurable to everyone. Sweetness itself, however, is pleasurable to all.

The Gita here not only says that all men, each in his own way, pursue some path to God. It also says the Lord *appears* to His worshipers. Thus, while guidance comes generally to all mankind through *karmic* law, devotees establish an inner, conscious relationship with the Lord.

Man first learns respect for the law. His respect evolves, in time, into divine devotion. Devotion, finally, attracts divine grace. God appears to His devotees, and reveals to them the truths of His eternal nature. In whatever form we worship God, and by whatever paths we strive to reach Him, He blesses us, eventually, with His bliss.

In this stanza we find a beautiful parallel to the verse in the Bible, "For the law was given by Moses, but grace and truth came by Jesus Christ." (John 1:17) The role of Jesus Christ, and also that of Krishna, is to bring souls back to union with God.

Thus, through the Bhagavad Gita, God has spoken to mankind.

Index of Scriptural Quotations

This index lists the Scriptural passages quoted in the text, in alphabetical order by scriptural location. The Bible quotations are listed first, followed by those from the Bhagavad Gita. Frequently, the passages have been abbreviated; you can find a more complete quotation in the text. A page number in **boldface** refers to a weekly commentary devoted to that quote.

Bible Quotations

John 1:17 "For the law was given by Moses, but grace and truth came by Jesus Christ." 195

John 4:13-14 "...Whosoever drinketh of this water shall thirst again..." 34, 37

John 4:24 "God is a Spirit..." 99

John 8:32 "...ye shall know the truth, and the truth shall make you free." 190

John 8:58 "...Before Abraham was, I am." 129

John 9:1-2 "...who did sin, this man, or his parents, that he was born blind?" 140, 150

John 9:3 "...Neither hath this man sinned, nor his parents: but that the works of God should be made manifest in him." 151

John 10:30 "I and my Father are One." 81

John 14:6 "...I am the way, the truth, and the life..." 33, **185**

John 14:12 "...the works that I do shall he do also..." 28

John 21:20-22 "...Lord, and what shall this man do?" 65

Luke 7:47 "...Her sins, which are many, are forgiven; for she loved much..." 150

Luke 9:49-50 "...he that is not against us is for us." **59**

Luke 15:11-24 "...A certain man had two sons..." **127**, 132

Luke 15:13 "...the younger son...took his journey into a far country, and there wasted his substance with riotous living." 133

Bhagavad Gita Quotations

Gita VI:27 "Supreme blessedness is that yogi's who has completely calmed his mind, controlled his ego-active tendencies (*rajas*), and purged himself of desire..." **132**

Gita VI:30-32 "One who beholds My presence everywhere,...He never loses loving sight of Me, Nor I of him, through all eternity...." **171**

Gita VI:37-47 "What is the fate of him who strives with faith, But fails, and loses heart; or even falls From holiness..." **163**

Gita VI:46 "Arjuna, be thou a yogi!" 104

Gita IX:1 "...To you, who are free from the carping spirit..." **53**

Gita IX:25 "Those who worship lesser gods go to their gods..." **91**

Gita XII:1-2,5 "...Those who, fixing their minds on Me, adore Me...are in My eyes the perfect knowers of yoga...." **101**

Gita XIII:7-11 "Humbleness, truthfulness, and harmlessness,...These qualities reveal true Wisdom, Prince." **73**

Gita XIV:24-25 "Unaffected by outward joys and sorrows, or by praise and blame..." **82**

A Selection of Other Books
by J. Donald Walters

Cities of Light — What Communities Can Accomplish, and the Need for Them in Our Times.

Intentional Communities — How to Start Them, and Why.

Crises in Modern Thought — Solutions to the Problem of Meaninglessness. This book probes the discoveries of modern science for their pertinence to lasting human values.

The Artist as a Channel — a book that proposes a new approach to the arts, one that combines deep, intuitive feeling with clear and meaningful insight.

The Search — A Young Person's Quest for Understanding. This autobiography is a deeply moving revelation of a poignant search for truth.

The Reappearance of Christ — The Scriptures as Messengers of Inner Communion. First of a three-volume series, with **Rays of the Same Light** Volumes II and III.

Rays of the Same Light — Parallel Passages, with Commentary, from the Bible and the Bhagavad Gita (Volume II).

The Art of Supportive Leadership — A Practical Handbook for People in Positions of Responsibility.

Education for Life — a book on childhood education.

The Story of Crystal Hermitage — the building of a home, and a life.

How To Be a Channel — how to truly transmit inspiration received from sources other than the ego.

Secrets of Happiness — One for Each Day of the Month.

Affirmations & Prayers — a collection of 52 spiritual qualities and a discussion of each, with an affirmation and prayer for its realization.

The Land of Golden Sunshine — a poetic parable.

On Wings of Joy — songs and poems of Divine Joy.

Ring, Bluebell, Ring! — Songs and Poems for Children Who Wonder.

J. Donald Walters lives at Ananda World Brotherhood Village, the spiritual community he founded in 1968. Ananda is one of the most successful intentional communities in the world. For further information about the community or its guest programs, or for a product brochure, please write the publisher, or call 916-292-3065.